KENTUCKY
ALWAYS IN SEASON

A Recipe Collection

by

Greta Hipp Burkhart

McClanahan
Publishing House

Cover design and book layout by James Asher Graphics

Manufactured in the United States of America

All book order correspondence should be addressed to:

McClanahan Publishing House, Inc.
P.O. Box 100
Kuttawa, KY 42055
270-388-9388
800-544-6959

www.kybooks.com
books@kybooks.com

Dedicated to my family—

my mother and grandmothers,
my father and grandfathers,
my husband and children

Introduction

"United We Stand, Divided We Fall," the creed of the Commonwealth of Kentucky applies to individuals as citizens of state and country. Its truth is also evidenced in the strength and happiness of families, which by circumstance, or conscious effort, remain close. A Kentucky family may be comprised of generations, young and old, and even friends "adopted" into the clan.

A Kentucky family's wealth lies in its written and verbal history, its promising future and a tradition of outstanding hospitality. While gathered around the table daily or on special occasions, family traditions are passed along. Friendly manners abound while tales of adventure are relayed. Cooks focus on preparing their best fare, while appreciative diners consume the bounty. Memories recall long afternoons spent chatting and resting in the shade after indulging in a picnic smorgasbord. Admiration for loving cooks enhance recollections of festive celebrations and holiday feasts.

No matter the weather or the time of year you are always welcome. Kentucky and her people are generous. Graced from region to region with unrivaled landscapes, from mountains to rivers, to rolling hills to fertile farmland, Kentuckians are blessed by their state's bounty. Kentucky produce and hickory smoked meats and it's legendary liquor, bourbon, are highly in demand. These have become ingrained in our culinary tradition, and are renowned throughout the country.

In this collection I offer a modest sampling of the foods that have to me become synonymous with times spent with loved ones. A desire to preserve beloved recipes while promoting healthful foods motivated me to write this cookbook. My grandmother's gentle instruction on food prepared from "scratch," combined with my mother's adaptation to modern conveniences have guided my interest in cooking. My personal contribution may be in devising resourceful ways to quickly prepare these dishes.

I sincerely hope you enjoy these recipes. May you and your family be blessed for many generations to come.

Always,

Greta Hipp Burkhart

Table of Contents

Acknowledgments

I would like to acknowledge the following for their influences on both my book and me. Heartfelt thanks to my mother, Jean Floyd Hipp, for her nurturing care throughout my life; to my grandmothers, Juel Winstead Hipp, and Mildred McMurtrie Floyd for their gift of making life wonderful and tender. I appreciate the strength and guidance of my father, Donald Martin Hipp, the memory of his father, Paul Hipp, and for the loving devotion of my grandfather, James Earl Floyd. My husband, Bruce Burkhart, contributed many hours of grilling and experimentation in helping with some recipes, and my children have been a joy to cook for! Thanks to my dear friends for the contribution of their recipes, Mrs. Edna Cooper Hipp, Mrs. Helen Bash, and Mrs. Ruth Yates. I also wish to extend thanks to Mrs. Paula Cunningham and Mrs. Michelle Stone, "The Cookbook Ladies," for their considerable assistance in creating and publishing this cookbook.

Appetizers
&
Beverages

Black-eyed Pea Dip

One 15-ounce can black-eyed peas, drained
½ cup plain nonfat yogurt
1 teaspoon chili powder
½ teaspoon garlic powder
¼ teaspoon ground red pepper
½ cup shredded low-fat Cheddar cheese
1 Tablespoon sliced green onions

Preheat oven to 400 degrees. Combine peas, yogurt, chili powder, garlic powder, and red pepper in blender or processor; blend until smooth. Coat 1-quart casserole with cooking spray. Spoon bean mixture into casserole. Bake at 400 degrees for 18 minutes; remove from oven, sprinkle with cheese. Return to oven and bake another 2-3 minutes. Sprinkle with onions before serving. Serve warm, with tortilla chips.

Simple Smoked Salmon Spread

One 7½ -ounce can red sockeye salmon, drained
8 ounces cream cheese, softened
Juice of one lemon, strained of seeds and pulp
1 Tablespoon prepared horseradish
½ teaspoon ground black pepper
½ teaspoon liquid smoke
½ teaspoon garlic salt
½ teaspoon ground cayenne pepper

Serve with saltines or savory crackers; also excellent as a spread on bagels or toast points for a light lunch.

Combine salmon and cream cheese with fork in mixing bowl. Add remaining ingredients to cheese mixture; blend thoroughly. Form into ball or form on a serving dish. Cover and chill in refrigerator, at least six hours, before serving.

Curried Spinach Ball

2 packages frozen chopped spinach,
thawed and squeezed dry
1 yellow onion, finely chopped
1 teaspoon cayenne pepper
2 Tablespoons mayonnaise
1 Tablespoon lemon juice
1 teaspoon curry powder

Mix all ingredients well. Shape into ball or roll. Chill in refrigerator
3 to 4 hours. Serve with wheat crackers.

Big Bleu Kentucky Cheese Ball

1 pound Bleu cheese
1 pound butter
½ cup bourbon
½ cup crushed toasted almonds
Fresh mint leaves

Wonderful with mild crackers, celery, or warm, toasted party rye bread.

Cream cheese together with butter in a large bowl. Slowly add bourbon while mixing. Add almonds, and form into a ball. Cover bowl lightly and refrigerate 24 hours. Serve on platter, garnished with fresh mint leaves.

12 servings

Lucky Cheese Pennies

1 stick margarine
8 ounces grated sharp Cheddar cheese
1 cup all-purpose flour
One 1-ounce envelope Golden Onion soup mix
½ teaspoon salt

Great to make ahead of serving time. Store these in an airtight container in the refrigerator and allow to reach room temperature before serving.

Allow margarine and cheese to soften to room temperature. Combine margarine and cheese in bowl, and mix thoroughly. Add flour and soup mix to cheese mixture, and mix to form a dough. Shape dough into a roll about 1-inch thickness. Slice into ¼-inch pieces and place on a baking sheet. Bake at 400 degrees for 7 minutes. Cool on rack before serving on tray.

50 to 60 pieces

Derby Day Cheese Straws

½ pound grated extra sharp Cheddar cheese
¼ pound butter, softened
½ teaspoon salt
⅛ teaspoon cayenne pepper
1½ cups self-rising flour

Combine all ingredients into a dough that is soft and pliable. A few drops of water may be added to improve dough. Roll out dough on a lightly floured board. Cut into strips with a sharp knife or pizza cutter. Place on a shiny ungreased baking sheet. Bake at 325 degrees for 20 minutes until straws begin to brown very lightly around the edges. Let cool on baking sheet. If desired, sprinkle lightly with paprika and salt. Store in airtight container between sheets of waxed paper.

This tasty recipe is taken from <u>Derby Entertaining,</u> another great cookbook from "The Cookbook Ladies" of McClanahan Publishing House.

6 dozen

Mother's Curried Cheese Puffs

36-40 green olives stuffed with pimentos
2 cups grated Cheddar cheese
1 stick margarine, not light or whipped
¼ teaspoon hot pepper sauce
1½ cup all-purpose flour
2 teaspoons curry powder
½ teaspoon salt

Preheat oven to 425 degrees. Drain olives and pat dry; set aside.
Blend cheese, margarine, and pepper sauce in a large mixing bowl.
Mix dry ingredients together in separate mixing bowl. Stir dry mix
into cheese mixture; work into a firm, smooth ball. Pinch off
enough dough to form into 1½-inch balls. Make deep impression
(with end of spoon or clean small finger) in center of each ball.
Insert an olive into each impression, with pimento end exposed.
Place balls on ungreased cookie sheet. Bake at 425 degrees for 15
to 18 minutes.

36 to 40 balls

Springtime Asparagus Puffs

8 ounces Bleu cheese Roquefort dressing
8 ounces cream cheese
1 egg, well beaten
1 large loaf sliced white bread
1 large can asparagus spears
4 Tablespoons melted butter

Preheat oven to 350 degrees. Blend cheese dressing, cream cheese and egg until smooth. Cut crust off each slice of bread. Roll each slice flat with rolling pin; spread cheese mixture on each slice. Place 1 asparagus spear on top of bread. Fold bread down, and cut into three parts. Brush with melted butter on all sides. Place on large cookie sheets. Bake at 350 degrees for 15 minutes. Broil for 1 or 2 minutes for a golden color.

Championship Bourbon Dogs

Bourbon dogs are a Kentucky twist to traditional beer dogs. They can be kept on low until all are devoured, and if the crowd you are serving grows, then add another package of miniature cocktail frankfurters to the simmering sauce.

One 14-ounce bottle of ketchup
1 cup bourbon
1 cup dark brown sugar
Four 8-ounce packages miniature cocktail frankfurters

Mix ketchup, bourbon, and sugar together in a crockpot. Cook on high heat until thoroughly heated. Reduce to low setting. Add franks, and cook for 30 minutes; stir occasionally. Serve "dogs" hot in a dish with some of the sauce, with toothpicks.

60 servings

Artichoke Stuffed Mushroom Caps

½ cup cooked white rice
One 6½-ounce jar artichoke hearts,
drained and finely chopped
1 Tablespoon mayonnaise
1 teaspoon Worcestershire sauce
20-24 large mushroom caps, cleaned and dry
20-24 slices pimento stuffed olives

This may be served as an appealing side dish as well.

Combine rice, artichoke hearts, mayonnaise, and Worcestershire sauce in bowl. Stuff each mushroom cap with rice mixture; top each with an olive slice. May be served hot or cold. To serve hot, broil briefly before serving; to serve cold, chill in refrigerator before serving.

Early Summer Bacon Wrapped Tomatoes

6 medium tomatoes
1 teaspoon Parmesan cheese
1 teaspoon salt
1 teaspoon basil
½ teaspoon black pepper
12 bacon slices, partially fried to soft stage, drained

Remove stems from tomatoes; cut each tomatoes ¾ way through to form 6 attached wedges. Combine cheese, salt, basil, and black pepper in small bowl. Spoon cheese mixture into each tomato. Wrap each tomato with two bacon slices, and secure with tooth-picks.

Place tomatoes in broiling pan. Sides should not be touching. Broil 5 to 10 minutes until tomatoes are tender. Be careful not to burn. Remove from broiler pan and pull out toothpicks. Serve on a warm dish.

6 servings

Edna's Green Pepper Jelly

6 large green peppers, stem and seeds removed
6 cups sugar
1½ cups white vinegar
6 ounces fruit pectin
1½ teaspoons hot pepper sauce
3 drops green food coloring

Sterilize four 8-ounce jelly glasses. Keep in hot water. Process green peppers until finely ground. Combine peppers, sugar, and vinegar in a large saucepan. Boil for 3 minutes. Remove from heat. Let stand for 5 minutes, then strain. Add fruit pectin, hot pepper sauce and food coloring; stir to mix. Spoon into jelly glasses, leaving a ½-inch edge from top. Cool and cover with aluminum foil and lids.

A delightful treat always given to us by my Aunt Edna Cooper Hipp at Christmas time, but which we enjoyed throughout the year. This is wonderful served with wheat crackers and cream cheese.

Jezebel

One 16-ounce jar pineapple preserves
Two 12-ounce jars apple jelly
One 6-ounce jar mustard
8 ounces prepared horseradish
1 Tablespoon sour cream
8 ounces cream cheese

Should pineapple preserves be difficult to find, substitute with 1 small jar pear or peach preserves, and 4 ounces crushed pineapple, drained.

Mix preserves, jelly, mustard, horseradish, and sour cream; blend well. Serve atop cream cheese, with variety crackers.

Welcome Retreat Baked Cheese with Tomato Chutney

1 egg
½ teaspoon ground red pepper
One 8-ounce round Farmers cheese
¼ cup toasted wheat germ
Tomato Chutney
French bread, sliced and toasted

Preheat oven to 375 degrees. Beat egg lightly, blend with red pepper. Dip cheese round in egg mixture. Coat dipped cheese round with wheat germ. Place on a baking sheet coated with spray. Loosely cover cheese round with aluminum foil which has been lightly sprayed with cooking spray on side toward cheese. Bake 10 minutes. Remove from oven, let stand for 5 minutes. Remove foil. Carefully transfer cheese round to serving plate. Serve warm, with Tomato Chutney and toasted French bread.

Tomato Chutney

One 14½-ounce can diced tomatoes
¼ cup water
2 Tablespoons red wine vinegar
2 Tablespoons sugar
¼ teaspoon ground ginger
¼ teaspoon ground cloves
⅛ teaspoon ground cinnamon
2 cloves garlic, minced
1 Tablespoon golden raisins

Combine tomatoes and juice from can, water, vinegar, sugar, ginger, cloves, cinnamon, and garlic in a saucepan; bring to a boil. Reduce heat and cook on low for 15 minutes, uncovered. Stir occasionally. Remove from heat, and stir in raisins; set aside. Serve warm.

Gracious Spiced Tea

A delicious drink to enjoy with friends or a quiet moment alone. Prepare mixture and put in a decorative jar with lid, label and give to a friend for a great personal gift.

1 cup instant tea mix
2 cups powdered orange drink
One 5-ounce package lemonade mix
1½ cups sugar
1 teaspoon ground cloves
1 teaspoon cinnamon
½ teaspoon allspice

Mix all ingredients together and store in container. Use 2 teaspoons mixture per 1 cup boiling water, when ready to serve.

Spring Morning Mimosas

4 cups chilled club soda
12-ounce can frozen orange juice concentrate
2 bottles chilled champagne

Blend 1 cup club soda and orange juice concentrate in blender. Pour into a punch bowl; stir in remaining club soda. Slowly add champagne. Float slices of orange if desired.

20 servings

Kentucky's Famous Mint Juleps

1 cup sugar
1 cup water
1 cup mint leaves
Crushed ice
100 proof bourbon
Mint sprigs

Combine sugar and water in a saucepan; bring to a boil. Cover and cook without stirring for 5 minutes. Remove from heat and allow to cool. Place mint in a bowl and bruise mint leaves with the back of a wooden spoon. Put mint and sugar mixture in a jar, cover, and chill 24 hours. Fill frosted silver julep cups or old-fashioned glasses with crushed ice. Pour 1 tablespoon strained sugar mixture and 1 ounce bourbon per serving. Garnish with a mint sprig.

Makes 21 servings.

Mock Mint Juleps

A refreshing alternative to traditional lemonade and mint julep.

4 mint sprigs
1½ cups sugar
2 cups cold water
¾ cup fresh lemon juice
1½ quarts ginger ale
Thin lemon slices

Rinse mint sprigs and discard stems. Place sugar, water, and lemon juice in bowl. Mix and stir in mint leaves. Allow to stand for 30 minutes. Fill a large pitcher with ice and stir liquid over ice. Add ginger ale and lemon slices. Pour into tall glasses.

Moonlight Punch

10 mint tea bags
2 cups boiling water
¾ cup sugar
One 6-ounce can frozen limeade concentrate
1 quart white grape juice
2 cups tonic water
1½ quarts lemon/lime soda
1 quart ginger ale
3 limes
Green maraschino cherries, for garnish
Fresh mint leaves, for garnish

A cool crowd pleaser! A dry ice mold placed in the center of the punch bowl gives this punch an ethereal appearance.

Steep tea bags in boiling water for 10 minutes. Remove tea bags; strain. Stir sugar into tea brew. Allow to completely cool. May be refrigerated, covered. Chill all ingredients. Pour tea mixture into 6-quart punch bowl. Add limeade concentrate, and stir to mix. Pour grape juice, tonic water, lemon/lime soda, and ginger ale into punch bowl. Stir slowly to mix. Slice limes thinly. Float several slices in punch. Place a lime slice, a green maraschino cherry, and a mint leaf in each glass.

25-30 servings

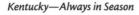

Blossom White Sangria

A refreshing variation to a classic red san-gria.

1 gallon Chablis
Juice of 1 lemon
Juice of 1 orange
Juice of 1 lime
10 fresh mint sprigs, washed
10 fresh strawberries, washed, stems and leaves removed
1 cup sugar

Combine all ingredients. Stir slowly until sugar is completely dissolved. Chill in covered container for 24 hours before serving. Strain if desired. Do not dilute.

Mama's Milk Toddy

1 cup milk, or half & half
1 Tablespoon powdered sugar
1 Tablespoon bourbon
1 teaspoon vanilla
1 cup ice cubes
Dash freshly grated nutmeg

Mix together first 4 ingredients in bowl. Add ice cubes, stir quickly. Strain into glass or mug. Dust with nutmeg.

Hearthside Hot Toddy

1 teaspoon honey
1 lemon slice
3 ounces bourbon
4 ounces boiling water
1 cinnamon stick

Put honey, lemon slice, and bourbon in large coffee cup. Pour in hot boiling water. Stir with cinnamon stick. Serve immediately.

Mim's Float

1 small package instant vanilla pudding
1 small package instant French vanilla pudding
1 cup sugar
½ gallon milk
Dash nutmeg
½ teaspoon vanilla extract
4½ ounces whipped topping

Mix pudding mixes, and sugar. Add milk slowly, then nutmeg and vanilla extract, if desired. Blend thoroughly. Add whipped topping. Keep refrigerated until ready to serve.

Welcome Home Wassail

This is a holiday tradition for Open House and Christmas Eve Dinner.

6 cups apple juice
2 cups cranberry juice cocktail
¼ cup sugar
1 stick cinnamon, broken into 1-inch pieces
6 whole cloves
1 teaspoon allspice
3 oranges
Extra whole cloves
1 teaspoon Angostura aromatic bitters
1 cup light rum

Combine liquids in large saucepan; heat on medium high heat. Add sugar, stir. Put cinnamon, 6 whole cloves, and allspice into tea caddy or cheesecloth bag. Drop spice bag into liquids. Bring to a boil, then reduce to simmer. Wash skins of whole oranges, then push whole cloves into skins to stud. Place studded oranges and bitters into liquids. Cover and simmer for 10 minutes. Add rum before serving. Serve hot.

10 to 12 punch cup servings

Breads
&
Brunch

Irish Soda Bread

2 cups whole-wheat flour
2 cups all-purpose flour
1 teaspoon baking powder
1⅓ teaspoons baking soda
½ teaspoon salt
2 Tablespoons granulated sugar
2 cups buttermilk

Combine wheat flour, and all-purpose flour in a large mixing bowl. Add baking powder, baking soda, sugar, and salt. Mix in buttermilk, and knead with hands until a soft wet dough forms. Turn out onto a lightly-floured board and knead just until dough sticks together. Form into a round loaf. Make some slits on the top of the loaf. Place on a lightly-greased baking sheet. Bake at 375 degrees for 20 to 25 minutes. Bread should be golden and insides thoroughly cooked. Serve hot.

Beer Bread

3 cups self-rising flour
3 Tablespoons sugar
1 can beer
1 Tablespoon melted butter

Preheat oven to 375 degrees. Lightly grease bread pan. Mix flour, sugar, and beer well. Put bread mixture into bread pan. Bake at 375 degrees for 1 hour. Remove from oven, brush with melted butter. Slice or serve on bread board with bread knife.

Hushpuppies

2 cups cornmeal
2 teaspoons baking powder
1 teaspoon salt
1½ cups milk
½ cup water
1 large yellow onion, finely chopped
Oil for frying

A traditional item served with catfish, cabbage slaw, and beans.

Sift together cornmeal, baking powder, and salt. Add milk and water to the mixture. Stir in onions and mix together well. Take dough by spoonfuls and form by hand into balls. Deep fry in hot oil until browned on each side, about 3 minutes total. Drain excess oil on paper towels. Serve hot.

Wildcat Cornbread

1 cup self-rising flour
2 cups self-rising cornmeal
¼ teaspoon salt
1 teaspoon sugar
½ cup vegetable oil
1 yellow onion, finely diced
One 14½-ounce can cream style corn
¼ cup diced green pepper
¼ cup diced red pepper
½ cup buttermilk
3 eggs, beaten

Sift flour into a large mixing bowl. Add cornmeal, salt, and sugar.
Stir to mix. Add oil, onion, corn, and peppers; then add milk and
eggs. Preheat oven to 400 degrees; place two greased iron skillets
in oven while heating. Pull out heated skillets, pour batter into
each evenly. Bake at 400 degrees for 35 to 40 minutes until golden
brown.

Kentucky Biscuits

2 cups all-purpose flour
2½ teaspoons baking powder
½ teaspoon baking soda
½ teaspoon salt
1 Tablespoon granulated sugar
½ cup butter
¾ cup buttermilk
1 Tablespoon melted butter

Mix flour, baking powder, baking soda, salt, and sugar in a bowl. Cut in butter with a pastry blender or knives until mixture resembles coarse crumbs. Add buttermilk and quickly mix to form a soft dough. Turn out onto lightly-floured board. Knead three times. Roll out to form a square an inch or so thick. Place on an ungreased baking sheet. Cut dough into 12 even biscuits, but do not separate. Brush with melted butter. Bake at 400 degrees for 15 minutes. Serve hot with butter, honey, jellies and jams.

Pecan Loaf

2 cups all-purpose flour
4 teaspoons baking powder
1 teaspoon salt
5 Tablespoons margarine
1 egg, beaten
1 cup milk
½ cup chopped pecans
2 teaspoons sugar

Mix and sift flour, baking powder, and salt in large bowl. Cut in margarine with fork or knives. Add beaten egg and milk. Stir in pecans and sugar. Turn into a buttered 10-inch loaf pan. Let stand 20 minutes. Bake at 350 degrees for 50 minutes.

May Day Bread

3 cups all-purpose flour, sifted
1 teaspoon baking powder
1 teaspoon salt
1 Tablespoon cinnamon
2 cups sugar
1¼ cups chopped pecans
4 eggs, beaten
1¼ cups vegetable oil
2 cups frozen sliced strawberries, thawed

This is wonderful spread with straw—berry butter or cream cheese, and is filled with a favorite spring fruit, STRAWBERRIES!

Sift together flour, baking powder, salt, cinnamon, and sugar in a large bowl. Combine pecans, eggs, oil, and strawberries in smaller bowl, mix well. Make a well in center of the dry mixture. Pour the pecan mixture into the well, and stir to moisten dry mixture thoroughly. Pour into greased 9 x 5 x 3-inch loaf pans. Bake at 350 degrees for 1 hour. Allow to cool 5 minutes before serving.

Pumpkin Pineapple Bread

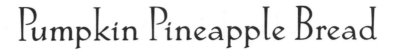

Topping

1 cup powdered sugar
1/4 cup pineapple juice
2 Tablespoons milk

Combine powdered sugar, juice, and milk in small mixing bowl. Stir with fork to make a thoroughly blended thin paste. Drizzle over warm bread, cake, or muffins.

1½ cups all-purpose flour
¼ cup firmly-packed brown sugar
2 heaping Tablespoons wheat germ
1 Tablespoon baking powder
½ teaspoon baking soda
¼ teaspoon ground cinnamon
1 cup pumpkin pie filling
8 ounces crushed pineapple, well drained, reserve pineapple juice for topping
2 Tablespoons canola oil
1 egg white

Combine flour, brown sugar, wheat germ, baking powder, baking soda, and cinnamon in a large mixing bowl. Mix together pumpkin pie filling, pineapple, oil and egg white in a separate mixing bowl. Stir pumpkin mixture until fluffy. Add pumpkin mixture to dry mixture and thoroughly blend. Pour into a 9 x 5-inch loaf pan that has been sprayed with cooking spray and lightly floured. Bake at 350 degrees for 50 minutes. Cool on wire rack about 15 minutes. Remove from pan if desired. Drizzle with topping while warm. Serve warm or chilled. Keeps well in refrigerator, covered.

Summertime Zucchini Bread

3 cups all-purpose flour
1 cup chopped walnuts
2 teaspoons baking soda
1½ teaspoons ground cinnamon
1 teaspoon salt
¾ teaspoon ground nutmeg
½ teaspoon baking powder
3 large eggs
1 cup light olive oil
2 cups sugar
2 teaspoons vanilla
2 cups shredded zucchini
One 8¼ -ounce can crushed pineapple, drained

Preheat oven to 350 degrees. Grease and flour two 8 x 4-inch loaf pans. Combine flour, nuts, soda, cinnamon, salt, nutmeg, and baking powder in medium bowl. In large bowl beat eggs at high speed. Beat in oil, sugar, and vanilla until mixture is thick and foamy. Stir in zucchini, pineapple, and flour mixture. Pour into loaf pans. Bake at 350 degrees for 1 hour. Let cool 10 minutes. Turn out onto wire racks.

Best Ever No-Fat Muffins

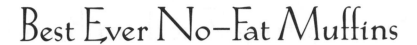

Lovely served with sugar-free, nonfat preserves.

1½ cups self-rising flour
¾ cup light brown sugar
½ cup peeled grated apple
2 teaspoons ground cinnamon
⅔ cup skim milk
⅔ cup plain, low-fat yogurt

Combine flour, sugar, apple, and cinnamon in large mixing bowl. Gently stir in milk and yogurt, until just mixed. Pour into 12 muffin tins which have been lightly coated with cooking spray. Bake at 400 degrees for 15 minutes.

A contribution from The Cookbook Lady of McClanahan Publishing House, Paula Cunningham.

Brown Sugar Muffins

½ cup butter
1 cup light brown sugar
1 egg, slightly beaten
1 teaspoon vanilla extract
1 cup milk
2 cups flour
1 teaspoon baking powder
1 teaspoon baking soda
Pinch salt
½ cup chopped nuts

Preheat oven to 350 degrees. Cream butter and sugar in large mixing bowl. Add egg, vanilla, and milk. Sift flour, baking powder, baking soda, and salt into bowl. Add nuts. Mix until ingredients are moist; spoon into muffin tins. Bake at 350 degrees for 15 to 20 minutes.

Makes 12 muffins.

Bridesmaids Brunch Cake

Glaze:

Combine powdered sugar and lemon juice. Stir until smooth.

2 cups yellow cake mix, sifted
½ cup sugar
2 Tablespoons poppy seeds
2 teaspoons baking powder
½ teaspoon ground cinnamon
⅛ teaspoon salt
8-ounce carton plain nonfat yogurt
¼ cup skim milk
¼ cup vegetable oil
1 egg, beaten
1 teaspoon almond extract
½ cup confectioner's sugar, sifted
2 teaspoons lemon juice

Preheat oven to 400 degrees. Lightly coat 9-inch baking pan with cooking spray. Combine cake mix, sugar, poppy seeds, baking powder, cinnamon, and salt in a large bowl; stir well. Combine yogurt, milk, oil, egg, and almond extract in bowl. Blend well. Add yogurt mixture to flour mixture. Stir until just moistened. Spoon batter into 9-inch square baking pan. Bake at 400 degrees for 20 minutes. Remove from oven; drizzle glaze over warm cake.

16 servings

Easy Biscuit Baklava

2 cans large flaky biscuits
1 stick butter, melted
1 cup finely chopped walnuts
1 cup honey

Coat 9 x 13-inch baking dish with cooking spray. Separate biscuits and peel each into four or five layers to total 45 layers. Place biscuit layers on bottom of baking dish in three rows of five. Brush with butter, and sprinkle with thin covering, approximately ⅓ cup, of nuts. Cover the layer with ⅓ cup honey. Repeat layer of biscuits, then butter, nuts, and ⅓ cup honey, twice. Bake at 325 degrees for 20 minutes. Do not allow to brown darkly or burn. Cool slightly before serving; best served at room temperature.

15 servings

Sunshine Soufflé

One 8-ounce carton frozen egg substitute
2 Tablespoons all-purpose flour
One 8-ounce carton lemon yogurt
6 egg whites, room temperature
1 teaspoon grated lemon rind
1 Tablespoon lemon juice
½ teaspoon cream of tartar
¼ cup sugar
2 teaspoons confectioner's sugar

This is a wel–comed surprise for guests; also makes a delightful dessert.

Preheat oven to 375 degrees. Coat 9 x 13-inch baking dish with cooking spray. In large mixing bowl beat egg substitute with mixer on high speed 5 minutes. Add flour and mix thoroughly. Stir in yogurt until mixed well. In separate large mixing bowl beat egg whites, lemon rind, lemon juice, and cream of tartar on high speed until soft peaks form. Add sugar to lemon mixture gradually, spoon at a time, while beating with mixer until stiff peaks form. Fold lemon mixture into yogurt mixture. Spoon mixture in 8 even mounds into baking dish. Bake at 375 degrees for 16 to 18 minutes. Remove from oven. Sprinkle lightly with powdered sugar. Serve immediately.

8 servings

A Real Man's Quiche

1 cup self-rising flour, sifted
⅓ cup cooking oil
3 Tablespoons milk
1 bunch green onions, minced
1 Tablespoon butter
4 slices bacon, cooked and broken
One 4-ounce can sliced mushrooms, drained
4 thin slices cooked ham, shredded
4 eggs
1½ cups evaporated milk
1 clove garlic, pressed
½ teaspoon dry mustard
½ teaspoon nutmeg
½ teaspoon ground black pepper
½ pound Swiss cheese, grated

Delicious served warm or cold.

In quiche pan combine flour, oil, and 3 Tablespoons milk. Mix thoroughly and press into bottom to form crust. Bake at 350 degrees for 3 to 5 minutes. Remove from oven, allow to cool. Sauté green onions in butter until tender. Layer bacon, mushrooms, ham, and onions on top of quiche crust. Beat eggs with milk and seasonings in small bowl. Pour over meat. Top with cheese. Bake at 350 degrees for 35 minutes.

6 to 8 servings

Sideboard Sausage Casserole

3 Tablespoons diced green pepper
½ yellow onion, diced
2 Tablespoons cooking oil
1 pound sausage, cooked, drained, crumbled
3 cups cooked brown rice
½ stick margarine
One 2-ounce jar diced pimento, drained
1 can water chestnuts, drained and finely chopped
½ teaspoon salt
½ teaspoon black pepper
1 can cream of Cheddar soup, undiluted
8 eggs

Sauté green pepper and onion in cooking oil. Combine sausage, rice, margarine, pimentos, water chestnuts, salt, black pepper, and soup in large mixing bowl. Add green peppers and onions to mixture. Mix well. Put in 9 x 13-inch buttered casserole dish and cover. Bake at 325 degrees for 25 minutes. Remove from oven, and with back of a large spoon make 8 indentations. Each indentation will serve as a cup for each egg. Break an egg into each cup. Loosely cover and return to oven to poach eggs to desired doneness.

8 to 10 servings

Tomato Cheese Toast

8 slices bread, lightly toasted
3 Tablespoons shredded Parmesan cheese
1 teaspoon lemon pepper
8 large round tomato slices, sliced ⅛-inch thick
10-ounce can of tender asparagus stems
1 cup shredded low fat Mozzarella

Best served warm.

Adding slices of turkey or ham to toast makes a hearty open–faced sandwich.

Lightly coat baking sheet with cooking spray. Position toast slices on baking sheet. Mix Parmesan cheese and lemon pepper thoroughly. Sprinkle each toast slice evenly with mixture. Place one tomato slice on each toast slice. Tomato should be large enough to almost cover surface of toast. Place 2 asparagus stems across each tomato slice. Top each tomato toast slice with shredded Mozzarella. Place baking sheet on oven rack raised to broiling level. Turn oven on to broil on low setting. Broil 3-4 minutes, cheese may be lightly browned in spots, but be careful not to let toast burn. Serve hot.

8 servings

Golden Garlic Grits

Grits
8-ounce package shredded Cheddar cheese
1 teaspoon minced garlic
4 eggs, beaten
1 cup milk or cream
½ teaspoon salt

I n the South grits
are served as a
side with shrimp.
Try them for meals
in addition to
breakfast or brunch!

Prepare grits as directed on box for six servings in large saucepan. Remove from heat. Stir in cheese, garlic, and salt. Mix eggs and milk together in small mixing bowl. Add egg mixture to grits slowly, stirring while adding. Pour grits into flat, buttered casserole dish. Bake at 350 degrees for 45 minutes until firm and browned slightly around edges.

8 servings

Salads
&
Soups

Sunshine Citrus Salad

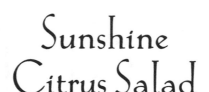

4 cups of lettuce and spinach leaves, washed, blotted,
and torn evenly
One 16-ounce can mandarin orange segments, drained
One 16-ounce can grapefruit segments, drained
½ green pepper, thinly slivered
One 4-ounce bag broken pecans or walnuts

Place salad leaves on individual salad plates. Center segments of
fruits on greens. Drizzle with salad dressing. Garnish with pepper
slivers and nuts.

Dressing

1 cup ranch dressing
½ cup honey

Combine in small bowl and stir vigorously. Drizzle lightly over citrus salad.

4 servings

Cherry Coke Salad

One 6-ounce jar maraschino cherries, chopped
One 8-ounce can crushed pineapple
Two 3-ounce packages cherry gelatin
Two 16-ounce bottles Coke
1 cup chopped black walnuts
One 3-ounce package cream cheese,
softened to room temperature

Drain fruit, pouring liquid into a small saucepan. Heat on medium heat and mix in gelatin. Remove from heat and let cool. Stir in Coke. When gelatin begins to thicken, add fruit, nuts, and cheese. Stir gently to mix. Chill until firm.

A soda fountain flavor that has been a favorite for gen— erations is passed along in this easy salad. My granddaddy, Earl Floyd, was employed by the Coca Cola Company of Kentucky for over fifty years.

8 servings

Cardinal Cranberry Salad

½ pound cranberries
2 seedless oranges, 1 peeled, 1 unpeeled
2 apples, cored and sliced, peeled if preferred
1 cup sugar
1 small package orange gelatin

Put cranberries, oranges, and apples in blender; grind until all processed. Add sugar, and then gelatin. Stir to thoroughly mix. Pour into serving dish. Cover and refrigerate. Serve when gelatin is set to desired consistency.

8 servings

Strawberry Pretzel Salad

2 cups coarsely crushed pretzels
¾ cup margarine
1 cup sugar plus 3 Tablespoons sugar, separated
1 large box strawberry gelatin
2 cups boiling water
Two 10-ounce packages frozen strawberries
One 8-ounce package cream cheese
One 8-ounce carton whipped topping

Spread crushed pretzels in bottom of 9 x 13-inch dish. Mix margarine and 3 Tablespoons sugar in small bowl. Sprinkle sugar mixture over pretzels. Bake at 400 degrees for 8 minutes. Cool thoroughly. Prepare gelatin with 2 cups boiling water. Stir in strawberries until berries become separated. Refrigerate gelatin mixture for 10 minutes. Blend cream cheese and 1 cup sugar in mixing bowl. Fold whipped topping into cream cheese mixture. Pour cream cheese mixture over pretzel crust. Carefully spoon strawberry gelatin mixture on top of cream cheese layer. Cover with cellophane and place in refrigerator at least one hour before serving.

Poison Salad

1 small box lime gelatin
One 3½-ounce can evaporated milk
½ cup salad dressing
2 celery stalks, diced
1 carrot, grated
1 small carton small curd cottage cheese

This surprising salad was named by my father, Donald Martin Hipp, who while courting my mother, Barbara Jean Floyd, attended a family dinner at her grandmother's home. My father really liked the green concoction that she had prepared, and when asking for a second serving he said, "Pass the Poison Salad, please." Our family has called it that ever since.

Prepare gelatin as directed on box. Chill to thickened but not firm consistency. Add evaporated milk, salad dressing, celery, carrot, and cottage cheese to gelatin. Mix thoroughly. Chill until firm.

Country Cornbread Salad

1½ cups chopped onion
1½ cups chopped green pepper
1 cup chopped whole sweet pickles, reserve pickle juice
One 4½ -ounce jar bacon bits
One 8-inch round cornbread, crumbled
1½ cups chopped fresh red tomatoes
One 15-ounce can red beans, drained
1½ cups salad dressing or mayonnaise

A great take to a potluck picnic!

Combine all ingredients except salad dressing or mayonnaise and pickle juice in bowl, and mix lightly with spoon. Thin salad dressing or mayonnaise with pickle juice and pour over cornbread mixture. Spoon into a serving dish, cover and refrigerate overnight before serving.

Jean's Steeped Slaw

This keeps well
while covered
and refrigerated.

One 16-ounce bag slaw mix
1 medium green pepper, thinly sliced
½ medium onion, chopped
One 4-ounce jar pimentos
½ cup water
¾ cup salad oil
¾ cup sugar
¾ cup white vinegar
1 teaspoon salt
1 teaspoon celery seed

Alternate slaw mix, green pepper, and onion in three layers, starting with slaw mix. Drain pimentos, put pimentos over top of slaw layers. Do not stir. Boil together water, oil, sugar, vinegar, salt, and celery seed for one minute. Pour over slaw mixture. Cover tightly. Refrigerate overnight.

12 to 15 servings

Complimentary Orange Relish

2 oranges
1 package fresh cranberries
1 cup sugar
1 small box orange gelatin

Remove membranes and seeds from oranges. Save juice and pulp of both oranges, and the outer rind of one orange with the bitter removed. Grind the cranberries, orange pulp, and orange rind in blender on high. Add sugar to cranberry mixture. Prepare the gelatin per package directions, leaving out the cold water. Combine cranberry mixture and gelatin together in bowl. Pour into serving dish, cover with cellophane, and chill in refrigerator 4 hours.

Dinnertime Apple Relish

3 cups cider vinegar
3 cups sugar
1 teaspoon celery seed
1 teaspoon salt
1 quart finely-diced red peppers
1 quart finely-diced green peppers
2 quarts peeled and finely-diced apples
1 quart diced, peeled yellow onion

A colorful and delicious treat for any occasion.

Combine vinegar, sugar, celery seed, and salt in 8-quart pan. Add peppers, apples, and onions. Bring to boiling and cook 15 minutes on high heat. Ladle into hot sterilized jars, and seal. Refrigerate after opening.

Piccalilli

8 cups quartered green tomatoes
4 cups cider vinegar, divided
6 green peppers, veins and seeds removed
6 red peppers, veins and seeds removed
4 medium onions, peeled and chopped
1 pint water
3½ cups sugar
¼ cup mustard seeds
¼ cup salt
2 Tablespoons celery seed
2 teaspoons allspice
1 teaspoon fresh ground cinnamon

A great treat at your table, or picnic, and a welcome gift. Shakers are credited for its name.

Completely chop tomatoes with 4 cups vinegar in blender. Pour into large stock pan or kettle. Completely chop peppers and onions, with water, in blender. Drain pepper mixture of excess liquid. Add to tomato mixture, and sugar and spices. Bring tomato mixture to a boil over high heat; reduce heat to medium and boil for 30 minutes. Stir frequently. Remove from heat and drain tomato mixture; discard liquid. Spoon mixture into canning jars and seal as jar manufacturer instructs.

Grandmother's Favorite Crisp Lime Pickles

Everything in my grandmother's garden grew prolifi-cally, especially cucumbers. These are easy to prepare, and are a great "snappy" pickle.

4 pounds cucumbers, sliced
1 cup lime powder
1 gallon water
1 quart vinegar
4½ cups sugar
½ teaspoon salt
1 Tablespoon pickling spices,
in tea ball or cheesecloth bag

Place cucumbers in solution of combined water and lime. Soak for 24 hours. Drain and rinse well with very cold water. Put cucumbers in very cold water and let stand for 6 hours. Rinse again. Put cucumbers in a large cooking pan. Add vinegar, sugar, salt, and pickling spices. Bring to a boil and simmer for 30 minutes. Pour into hot sterilized jars and seal.

Kentucky Burgoo

1 chicken for stewing
2 pounds beef loin
1½ pounds mutton
½ veal shoulder
2 ham hocks
Water
4 Tablespoons ground black pepper
4 large stalks celery, finely chopped
7 large carrots, finely chopped
One 28-ounce can cut green beans
2 large green peppers, veins and seeds removed, chopped
2 large yellow onions, finely chopped
6 large potatoes, peeled and chopped
One 16-ounce bag frozen green peas
One 16-ounce bag frozen yellow corn
Three 15-ounce cans crushed tomatoes
¾ cup Worcestershire sauce
2 cups catsup
¼ cup vinegar

Place meats in a large stock pan, cover with water and season heavily with black pepper. Cook over medium-high heat until meat is tender. When meat is pulled with a fork it should be stringy. Take out meat piece by piece, remove bones and cut meat into small bites. Discard bones and return meat to broth. Add remaining ingredients, and cook over medium heat until vegetables are tender. Reduce heat and cover. Stir occasionally to prevent from burning. Serve hot with cornbread or table bread.

Blackberry Soup

2 cups seedless blackberries, fresh or frozen
Two 6-ounce cans frozen apple juice concentrate, thawed
¼ teaspoon ground cinnamon
Dash ground nutmeg
¼ cup water
1 Tablespoon cornstarch
1 teaspoon vanilla extract

A cold spell in May, called "blackberry winter," predicts the crop which is ready to pick by the fourth of July. A distinctly flavored berry, the seedless variety should be used in this recipe.

Combine blackberries, apple juice concentrate, cinnamon, and nutmeg in a large saucepan. Bring to a boil, stirring constantly. Reduce heat and simmer 5 minutes, stirring occasionally. Combine water and cornstarch, stirring until smooth. Add cornstarch mixture to blackberry mixture in saucepan. Increase heat slightly to cook, stirring constantly, for 1 minute. Remove from heat. Stir in vanilla. Let cool. Chill in refrigerator, covered, for 8 hours. Serve cold, with light crackers.

6 to 8 servings

Watermelon Soup

2 cups peeled watermelon, cubed and seeded
1 cup half and half
¼ cup sugar
½ teaspoon salt
½ cup white wine
Fresh mint sprigs

Combine watermelon, half and half, sugar, salt, and wine in blender.
Process until thoroughly blended. Pour into chilled soup bowls.
Garnish each bowl with a fresh mint sprig.

6 servings

One of a Kind Soup

1 medium potato
1 medium onion
1 medium apple
1 medium banana
1 celery heart with leaves
1 pint chicken consommé
1 teaspoon salt
1 cup half & half
1 Tablespoon butter, melted
1 teaspoon curry powder
1 teaspoon ground black pepper
1 Tablespoon chopped chives

Peel and coarsely chop vegetables and fruit. Combine and simmer in salted chicken consommé in large saucepan on low heat until potato is soft. Blend until smooth. Stir in half & half, butter, curry powder, and pepper. Remove from heat. Chill covered for 4 hours in refrigerator. Serve in chilled bowls, and top with chopped chives.

4 servings

Red Onion Soup

5 cups thinly sliced red onions
3 Tablespoons butter
3 Tablespoons all-purpose flour
½ cup bourbon
2 quarts beef broth
¼ teaspoon basil
8 slices French bread, toasted
8 slices Swiss cheese

A rich soup to warm the soul, and to share with friends.

Sauté onions in butter in a heavy saucepan over medium-low heat until transparent. Stir in flour with a fork, making a paste. Pour in bourbon and beef broth; season with basil. Reduce heat to simmer, and cook 30 minutes. Place one slice of bread per serving in bottom of ovenproof bowl. Ladle onion soup, approximately ¾ cup, onto bread. Cover with a cheese slice. Broil in oven on low, until cheese is bubbly. Serve while hot.

8 servings

Amish
Tomato Noodle Soup

The Amish have enriched Kentucky's culture. The Amish provide fresh produce, baked goods, and dairy products at nearby markets and for visitors to their communities.

One quart pureed tomatoes
or one 28-ounce can crushed tomatoes
2 cups water
½ cup butter
One 8-ounce package egg noodles
1 quart milk
1 pint half & half
½ teaspoon salt
1 Tablespoon sugar

In large saucepan bring tomatoes and water to a boil. Add the butter and noodles, simmer 20 minutes until noodles are tender. Reduce heat to low, add milk and cream, stirring constantly to prevent from scalding. Add salt and sugar. Serve while hot.

12 servings

Ham 'n Pea Soup

2 cans green pea soup
2 cans water
2 cups sliced and chopped celery
2 cups sliced and chopped onion
2 cups sliced and chopped carrots
1 can sliced mushrooms, undrained
2 cups ham, cooked and cubed
2 teaspoons Italian dressing
2 teaspoons parsley flakes
¼ teaspoon black pepper
2 teaspoons chicken bouillon granules
1½ teaspoons seasoning salt
½ teaspoon powdered garlic
1 teaspoon oregano
10 drops hot pepper sauce

Excellent with cornbread!

Heat soup and water in 2-quart saucepan to medium-high heat.
Add celery, onion, and carrots to soup. Cook until tender. Add
mushrooms with liquid, ham and seasonings. Cover and simmer
15 minutes, stirring occasionally. Serve warm.

Polska Potato Soup

A delicious soup devised by my mother Jean Floyd Hipp for the enjoyment of her dinner guests and, of course, my father.

1 clove garlic, crushed
1 medium yellow onion, chopped
1 Tablespoon margarine
6 cups water
4 chicken bouillon cubes
3 medium russet potatoes, cut into ½-inch cubes
2 medium carrots, thinly sliced
2 stalks celery, with tops, sliced
1 teaspoon dried dill weed
½ teaspoon black pepper
One 6-inch Polska Kielbasa sausage, cut into ¼-inch slices

Sauté garlic and onion in margarine until onion is transparent; set aside. Bring water to a boil in stock pan. Add bouillon cubes and dissolve completely. Lower heat and add the onion, garlic, and remaining ingredients except the sausage. Cover and cook over medium heat until potatoes and carrots are almost tender. Do not stir while cooking. Add the sausage and cover. Simmer until the meat is thoroughly heated and potatoes are tender.

6 to 8 servings

Entrées

Autumn Apple Chicken

Best served while hot.

4 chicken quarters
1 cup apple cider
½ cup all-purpose flour
1 teaspoon ground ginger
1 teaspoon cinnamon
½ teaspoon salt
½ teaspoon pepper
2 Tablespoons brown sugar
1 apple, cored and sliced
2 Tablespoons honey

Place chicken quarters in shallow baking dish. Pour apple cider over chicken and cover with cellophane wrap. Marinate for 1 hour in refrigerator. Remove the chicken from cider; reserve the cider. Mix the flour, ginger, cinnamon, salt, and pepper in a small bowl. Dredge the chicken in the flour mixture. Return the chicken to the baking dish, skin side up. Bake at 350 degrees for 40 minutes. Combine reserved cider, brown sugar, apple slices, and honey. Pour over chicken, and bake another 20 minutes.

Golden Honey Chicken

6 chicken breasts, skinned
6 Tablespoons margarine
¼ cup Dijon mustard
2 teaspoons salt
2 teaspoons curry powder
1 cup honey

Place chicken in large casserole dish. Melt margarine in small saucepan on low heat. Add mustard, salt, curry powder, and honey to saucepan. Stir to blend. Pour butter mixture over chicken breasts, coating both sides well. Bake at 350 degrees for 30 minutes, basting occasionally. Cover and bake an additional 15 to 30 minutes.

6 servings

Sunshine Chicken

6 to 8 chicken breasts
One 18-ounce bottle barbecue sauce
1 Tablespoon Worcestershire sauce
¼ cup orange juice
½ cup brown sugar
1 grapefruit
1 orange
1 lemon

Chicken will be delight-fully tender and moist. Pork chops may also be pre-pared with this recipe.

Place chicken breasts, meat side down in 9 x 13-inch casserole sprayed lightly with cooking spray. Combine barbecue sauce, Worcestershire sauce, orange juice, and brown sugar in small bowl. Slice grapefruit, orange, and lemon in thin round slices with rinds, removing seeds. Layer fruit slices over chicken to cover, and secure with toothpicks. Pour barbecue sauce mixture over entire casserole ingredients. Lift chicken breasts with fork to allow sauce to get beneath breasts. Bake at 350 degrees for 1 hour and 45 minutes to 2 hours. Baste with its juices every thirty minutes. Remove toothpicks before serving. Citrus may be eaten.

6 to 8 servings

No Fuss Turkey

One 3-pound boneless turkey breast
1 cup water
2 to 3 large carrots, pared and cut
2 large celery stalks, chopped
½ teaspoon salt
½ teaspoon pepper

Exceptionally tender meat, and delicious carrots. Serve with Traditional Cornbread Dressing.

Place turkey in crockpot. Add water. Turn on to High setting until water is very hot. Add carrots, celery, salt, and pepper. Reduce to low setting and cover. Let cook undisturbed for three hours.

6 to 8 servings

Kentucky Hot Brown

8 slices toast with crust trimmed off
1 pound cooked white turkey breast, thinly sliced
½ pound cooked cured ham, thinly sliced
4 thick slices tomato
8 thick-sliced bacon strips, partially cooked
4 ounces grated Parmesan cheese

Cut toast into triangles and place in 9 x 13-inch baking dish. Place turkey and ham slices on toast. Cover with hot cheese sauce. Top with tomato slices and bacon strips. Sprinkle with Parmesan cheese. Bake at 425 degrees until bubbly.

Hot Cheese Sauce

2 Tablespoons butter
¼ cup all-purpose flour
2 cups milk
¼ cup grated sharp Cheddar cheese
¼ cup grated Parmesan cheese
¼ teaspoon salt
½ teaspoon Worcestershire sauce

Melt butter in saucepan. Add flour and stir well. Add milk, cheeses, salt, and Worcestershire sauce. Cook over medium low heat; stirring constantly, until thick. Use sauce as hot brown topping for toast and turkey slices.

Bluegrass Baked Ham and Greens

5 pound cooked ham
1 teaspoon liquid smoke
1 cup dark brown sugar
½ cup finely-chopped green pepper
1 cup apple juice
2 pounds kale or greens
8 stalks green onions

Cut ham in half and fit into large casserole dish. Puncture ham with fork. Combine liquid smoke, brown sugar, green pepper, and apple juice in bowl. Pour liquid smoke mixture over ham. Cover and bake at 325 degrees for two hours. Uncover and baste ham every 30 minutes with liquids in baking dish to keep ham moist. During last 30 minutes of baking ham: Clean fresh kale or greens thoroughly with running water. Chop kale or greens finely and place in boiling water for 15 minutes. Drain. Chop green onions finely and stir into cooked kale or greens. Remove ham from oven. Cut deep slits in top of ham with a long sharp knife. Stuff greens mixture into slits, and baste with liquid juices in baking dish. Cover; return to oven and continue to bake at 325 degrees for another 30 minutes. Serve ham sliced with greens while warm.

10 to 12 servings

Winter's Evening Wine Baked Ham & Round Steak

3 Tablespoons cooking oil
6 small whole onions
1 ham steak, cubed in 1-inch pieces
1 medium round steak, trimmed, but not tenderized
Flour
Salt
Red wine
Butter
Pepper
Basil leaves
Arrowroot or cornstarch

Coat iron skillet with oil, heat on medium high heat. Brown onions in skillet. Add ham to skillet and cook over medium heat. Dust steak with flour and salt on both sides. Remove ham and onions from skillet and set aside. Add wine to skillet to deglaze. Add small amount of oil or butter to skillet and then add steak. Brown steak on both sides. Put ham and onions on top of steak. Add enough wine to cover meat. Sprinkle with pepper and basil. Cover tightly with lid. Bake at 350 degrees for 1½ hours. Slice beef diagonally, place on platter, top with ham and onions. Thicken pan drippings with arrowroot or cornstarch. Pour over meats.

6 servings

Potluck Pork Chops with Sauce

2 Tablespoons all-purpose flour
¼ teaspoon salt
⅛ teaspoon pepper
8 center loin pork chops, lean, boned
1 teaspoon olive oil
4 ounces frozen orange juice concentrate, thawed
2 Tablespoons lemon juice
2 Tablespoons minced green onions
2 Tablespoons Dijon mustard
1 teaspoon brown sugar
1 teaspoon dried whole basil
¼ teaspoon curry powder
Dash of red pepper

Delicious!

Combine flour, salt, and pepper in a small bowl. Stir well. Dredge chops in flour mixture. Coat a large skillet with cooking spray and add oil. Heat on medium-high heat. Cook chops on each side 3 to 5 minutes. Add orange juice concentrate and lemon juice to skillet. Cook another 5 minutes until tender. Remove chops from skillet; keep warm. Serve with sauce.

Sauce

Add onions, mustard, brown sugar, basil, curry powder, and red pepper to skillet with juices. Cook over medium heat 1 minute until thickened; stirring frequently. Spoon over warm chops.

4 to 8 servings

Rainy Day Spicy Linguine

1 pound sage or hot pork sausage
¼ cup olive oil
1 medium eggplant, peeled and diced
2 Tablespoons water
One 8-ounce package linguine
½ cup minced parsley

Brown sausage in olive oil in 4-quart saucepan over medium-high heat. Break apart sausage while cooking. Remove from pan and drain. Cook the eggplant in the saucepan with sausage drippings and water over medium-high heat until eggplant is tender; drain. Prepare linguine according to package directions. Drain and keep linguine warm. Add cooked eggplant to the linguine in saucepan, then add parsley and sausage meat. Toss and serve on warmed serving platter.

4 servings

Hearty Kraut Sandwiches

2 large links smoked sausage
One 14-ounce can sauerkraut
2 Tablespoons stone ground mustard
½ teaspoon caraway seeds
4 Kaiser rolls, halved and toasted
8 ounces Havarti or Farmer's cheese, thinly sliced

Slice sausages in ¼-inch round slices and brown in skillet over medium heat. Top sausages with sauerkraut and turn with spatula until evenly mixed. Cover with lid and reduce heat to medium low for 10 minutes. Spread mustard on upper halves of rolls after arranging open faced on broiler rack. Using slotted spoon top each slice with sausage and sauerkraut. Sprinkle with caraway seeds, and cover with sliced cheese. Broil for 15 seconds, until cheese is melted. Remove from oven and serve open faced while hot.

4 servings

Great Aunt Helen's Meatloaf

My grand-mother's sister, Helen McMurtrie Bash, contributes this prize–winning recipe. It truly is great and is lovingly served with the family meal and as a potluck favorite.

1 pound lean ground beef
1 cup Grapenuts flakes
1 egg, beaten
1 cup milk
1 Tablespoon horseradish
¼ cup minced onion
¼ cup chopped green pepper
1¼ teaspoon salt
½ teaspoon black pepper
1 Tablespoon sugar
4 Tablespoons ketchup

Combine all ingredients except ketchup. Form into loaf, place in 9 x 5 x 3-inch loaf pan. Bake at 375 degrees for 1 to 1¼ hours. Drain excess juices during baking. Last 15 minutes of baking spread 4 tablespoons ketchup over top.

Ohio River Chili

2 pounds ground beef
2 medium onions,
ends and outer skins removed, chopped
1 quart water
One 14½-ounce can diced tomatoes
1½ teaspoons white vinegar
1 teaspoon Worcestershire sauce
2 teaspoons ground cumin
1½ teaspoons allspice
1½ teaspoons salt
1 Tablespoon chili powder
1 teaspoon cayenne
1 teaspoon cinnamon
½ teaspoon garlic powder
2 Tablespoons cocoa powder
2 bay leaves

"3–way" Serve on spaghetti and top with cheese.

"4–way" Serve on spaghetti and top with cheese and onions.

"5–way" Serve on spaghetti and beans and top with cheese and onions.

Combine beef, onions, and water in saucepan. Simmer until beef turns brown. Add tomatoes with liquid. Add remaining ingredients. Simmer for 3 hours. Stir occasionally to mix flavors, but not too frequently. Allow to rest, then skim off fat. Serve very warm, with or without toppings.

Toppings

1½ cups shredded Cheddar cheese
1 cup chopped onion
16 ounces canned kidney beans
Spaghetti, cooked and drained

Fisherman's Favorite Shrimp-stuffed Catfish

Very nice served with rice.

2 cups cooked and peeled fresh shrimp
2 eggs
1 cup half & half
½ cup cooking sherry
½ cup chopped green onions
2 Tablespoons chopped parsley
½ cup chopped mushrooms
1 teaspoon salt
1 teaspoon ground black pepper
½ teaspoon paprika
12 large catfish filets
Lemon wedges

Mince shrimp. Combine shrimp with eggs, half & half, sherry, onions, parsley, mushrooms, salt, pepper, and paprika in bowl. Place 6 catfish filets in 9 x 13-inch casserole dish lightly sprayed with cooking spray. Spoon shrimp mixture evenly onto filets. Top with 6 remaining filets. Bake at 350 degrees for 45 minutes. Serve with lemon wedges.

6 servings

Father's Day Garlic Butter Shrimp

3 pounds uncooked fresh shrimp in shells, 31-35 count
1 stick butter
1 Tablespoon ground black pepper
1 large bottle Italian dressing
Juice of 4 lemons
4 garlic cloves, crushed

Preheat oven to 350 degrees. Layer shrimp in large roasting dish. Melt butter in saucepan on low heat. Add pepper, dressing, lemon juice, and garlic to butter. Pour garlic butter over shrimp. Cover with pan lid or heavy foil. Bake at 350 degrees for 40 minutes. Serve hot.

Serve with hot crusty bread, and use garlic butter for dipping. Provide a side bowl for dis— carded shrimp peels. Slice lemons and place in side bowls with warm water, as finger bowls.

6 to 8 servings

Tuesday Tuna Roll

Crust

1 cup sifted all-purpose flour
⅓ cup shortening
¼ cup grated Cheddar cheese
½ teaspoon salt
3 to 4 Tablespoons water

Place flour and shortening into large mixing bowl. Cut flour and shortening with crossed knives into pea size pieces. Stir cheese and salt in with flour mix using a fork. Add water, stirring until mixture forms a ball. Chill in refrigerator for 15 minutes. Roll into a 9 x 13-inch rectangle on a piece of floured wax paper.

Filling

2 Tablespoons chopped onion
2 Tablespoons butter or margarine
1 large can of tuna, drained
1 Tablespoon all-purpose flour
¼ cup milk
¼ teaspoon salt
½ teaspoon marjoram
½ teaspoon thyme
1 egg, beaten, reserving 1 Tablespoon of egg to top crust

Cook onion in butter in skillet over medium-low heat until transparent. Add tuna, heat thoroughly. Mix flour, milk, salt, marjoram, thyme, and egg into tuna mixture. Stir while cooking until thickened. Remove from heat to cool. When mixture is cooled, spread evenly down center of crust rectangle to within 1½ inches of ends. Fold ends up and over filling. Moisten side edges with small amount of water, fold toward middle. Lap edges to form seam down middle and over ends. Flip onto baking sheet, seam side down. Prick top of crust with fork, brush with reserved egg. Bake at 350 degrees for 40 to 45 minutes.

4 to 6 servings

Lakeside Baked Crappie

8 crappie fish filets, rinsed and completely de-boned
3 potatoes, peeled, thinly-sliced into rounds
3 lemons, washed, thinly-sliced cross cut, de-seeded
1 large yellow onion, sliced into thin rings
4 Tablespoons butter or margarine
2 teaspoons lemon pepper
½ teaspoon salt

Preheat oven to 300 degrees. Cut 8 foil pieces, each large enough to wrap one filet completely plus fold. Place one filet in the center of each foil piece. Layer potato rounds from one end to the other on the filet. Repeat per fish. Layer several thin lemon slices on potato layer. Repeat per fish. Dot each fish with approximately ½ Tablespoon butter. Sprinkle each fish with lemon pepper and salt. Wrap and seal each fish and layers in foil packets. Bake at 300 degrees for 20-25 minutes. Remove from oven; open packets carefully. Serve hot.

8 servings

Veggie Lover's Fried Rice

3 teaspoons vegetable oil, divided
¾ cup diagonally-sliced celery
½ cup diagonally-sliced carrot
1 small sliced onion
1 Tablespoon minced ginger
1 clove garlic
½ cup fresh sliced mushrooms
8-ounce can bamboo shoots, drained
3 cups cooked brown rice
1 egg, lightly beaten
3 Tablespoons soy sauce
3 Tablespoons dry sherry
2 Tablespoons sliced green onions

Coat wok or skillet with cooking spray. Add 2 teaspoons oil to wok, coating sides. Place over medium-high heat until hot. Stir fry celery, carrots, onion, ginger, garlic, mushrooms, and bamboo shoots for 2 minutes. Stir in cooked rice until combination is thoroughly heated. Push rice mixture to sides forming a well in the center. Add 1 teaspoon oil, and beaten egg into well. Cook until egg is lightly set; stir in rice mixture. Add soy sauce and sherry, stirring constantly. When completely combined, top with green onions and serve.

6 to 8 servings

Garden Fresh Pasta Primavera

¼ cup margarine
2 cups broccoli flowerets, small pieces
1 cup thinly sliced, diagonally-cut carrots
½ cup sliced green onions
2 cloves garlic
1 Tablespoon basil
2 cups sliced fresh mushrooms
¼ teaspoon salt
¼ teaspoon pepper
½ cup Chablis
One 8-ounce package angel hair pasta,
cooked and drained
3 Tablespoons grated Parmesan cheese

Melt margarine in large skillet over medium heat. Sauté broccoli, carrots, green onions, garlic, and basil for 5 minutes, stirring frequently. Add mushrooms, salt, pepper, and wine, cook until mushrooms are tender. Add cooked pasta to warm. Transfer to serving dish and toss with cheese.

8 servings

Sides

Baked Cinnamon Apples

6 medium apples
½ cup brown sugar
½ stick margarine
¼ teaspoon allspice
½ teaspoon cinnamon
⅛ teaspoon cloves
⅛ teaspoon salt
½ cup cinnamon candies
½ cup raisins

Choose firm baking apples. Core and remove ½ inch peel from top. Place open end up in baking dish. Mix sugar, margarine, spices and salt in small bowl. Fill apple centers halfway with mixture, reserving ¼ mixture for topping. Stuff cinnamon candies and raisins into apple centers. Top apple centers with remaining sugar mix; pack down. Bake at 325 degrees for approximately 30 minutes. Apples should be bubbly and tender, but not mushy. Serve in separate dishes. May be topped with heavy cream.

6 servings

Gala Fruit Compote

One 15-ounce can pear halves
One 15-ounce can pineapple chunks
½ cup brown sugar
1 Tablespoon curry
One 15-ounce can peach halves
One 6-ounce jar maraschino cherries
¼ cup melted butter

An elegant southern dish, this curried compote is beautifully served with our finest silver.

Preheat oven to 325 degrees. Arrange fruit in a shallow dish. Mix sugar, curry, and butter; sprinkle over the fruit. Bake at 325 degrees for 30 to 45 minutes.

Barbecued Succotash

1 Tablespoon diced onion
2 teaspoons diced green pepper
¼ cup tomato sauce
3 Tablespoons vinegar
1 Tablespoon brown sugar
1 Tablespoon Worcestershire sauce
½ teaspoon chili powder
2 teaspoons yellow mustard
One 10-ounce package frozen baby lima beans,
thawed, drained
½ cup frozen whole kernel corn, drained

Coat skillet with cooking spray. Place on medium-high heat. Sauté onion and green pepper in skillet until tender. Stir in tomato sauce, vinegar, brown sugar, Worcestershire sauce, chili powder, mustard. Reduce heat to simmer. Stir in beans and corn. Bring to a boil; stirring occasionally. Cover skillet and reduce heat. Simmer 10 minutes.

4 to 6 servings

Carrot Vinaigrette

8 carrots, pared and julienned
¼ cup water
2 Tablespoons tarragon vinegar
1 teaspoon salt
1 teaspoon sugar
½ teaspoon fresh lemon juice
2 Tablespoons salad oil
⅛ teaspoon black pepper, preferably freshly ground
¼ teaspoon dried dill
2 Tablespoons chopped fresh green onions

Place carrots and water in flat saucepan. Cover and cook on low heat for 15 to 20 minutes. Remove from heat and drain. Combine all other ingredients in large bowl. Add carrots to bowl and mix well. Cover and refrigerate for 4 hours.

8 servings

Thunder 'n Lightning

3 medium tomatoes
1 large yellow or Vidalia onion
2 large cucumbers
One 14-ounce bottle Zesty Italian salad dressing
1 cup ice

A must have for picnics, this zesty dish proves tomatoes and cucumbers go together like thunder 'n lightning.

Peel and core tomatoes. Slice into bite size wedges. Place in 2 - quart or larger container. Remove ends and outer skins from onion. Slice thinly. Place in container with tomatoes. Remove ends and skin from cucumbers. Cross cut thinly into round bite size pieces. Place in container with tomatoes and onion. Shake bottle of dressing well; pour over combined slices. Stir to coat all pieces. Add ice to mixture and stir to combine. Cover with lid and refrigerate 2 hours. Stir before serving.

10-12 servings

Fresh Green Beans

2 pounds fresh green beans
1 medium yellow onion, ends and outer skin removed
4 cups water
4 beef bouillon cubes
1 slice hickory smoked bacon

Wash beans thoroughly, dry. Snap off ends of beans, and pull off string, if using string beans. Discard ends and strings. Use beans whole or snap each into two or three pieces, depending on preference and size of beans. Place bacon in bottom of large cooking pot. Turn burner heat on high. When bacon begins to sweat, put beans, water, and whole onion in pot. Bring water to a boil, then add bouillon cubes. Stir to blend flavors. Cover and reduce heat to low. Allow to cook down, about 35 to 45 minutes. Remove onion before serving.

Green beans are a staple in Kentucky. Gardeners dedicate rows to the many varieties, like the Kentucky Wonder beans. The green bean is the favorite vegetable of the children (some grown, including myself) in my family.

8 servings

Easy Stuffed Mushrooms

30 medium fresh mushrooms
½ cup shredded Mozzarella cheese
¼ cup oil-free Italian dressing
1 teaspoon minced fresh garlic

Preheat oven to 350 degrees. Clean mushrooms with damp paper towels; remove stems. Chop stems into small pieces. Combine stems, cheese, dressing, and garlic in a bowl; stir well. Spoon mixture into mushroom caps. Place in shallow baking dish. Bake at 350 degrees for 15 to 20 minutes.

Golden Rice

1 large golden delicious apple, cored and cubed
3 tablespoons butter
½ teaspoon curry powder
3 cups cooked long-grain white rice

Cook apple in skillet with butter and curry over medium heat for 5 minutes. Stir cooked apples into rice and mix well. Serve while hot.

6 servings

Lady's Okra & Tomatoes

¼ cup olive oil
3 cups fresh okra, sliced
1 large tomato, peeled and chopped
1 Tablespoon Italian seasoning
½ teaspoon salt
½ teaspoon lemon juice

Delicious hot or cold.

Heat olive oil in large skillet to medium-high, do not allow to smoke. Put okra in skillet, stir fry. Reduce heat. Add tomato to skillet and allow to cook until hot. Stir in seasoning and salt, then stir in lemon juice until combined thoroughly. Cover and simmer five minutes.

6 to 8 servings

Candied Sweet Potatoes

6 large sweet potatoes
1 quart water
1 teaspoon salt
½ cup packed brown sugar
1 stick margarine, cut in small pieces

Wash and place whole sweet potatoes with skins in 4-quart saucepan. Cover with water and heat to boiling. Reduce heat and simmer 30 minutes, until potatoes are tender. Drain and allow potatoes to cool enough to handle. Remove peels from potatoes and cut into ¼-inch thick slices. Arrange half the slices in a 9 x 13-inch baking dish which has been lightly sprayed with cooking spray. Salt the slices and sprinkle with half the brown sugar and half the margarine pieces. Repeat with the remaining potato slices, salt, brown sugar, and margarine. Cover dish and bake at 325 degrees for 45 minutes.

10 servings

Classic Corn Pudding

Two 8-ounce cans cream-style corn
¼ cup all-purpose flour
1 teaspoon salt
1 Tablespoon honey
2 Tablespoons melted butter
2 eggs, beaten
2 cups milk

Combine corn, flour, salt, honey, and butter in large bowl.
Combine eggs and milk in separate bowl. Beat together well. Stir
egg mixture into corn mixture. Mix well. Pour into casserole dish
sprayed with cooking spray. Bake at 350 degrees for 30 minutes.
Stir once or twice during baking to prevent corn from settling.

Broccoli Rice Casserole and its Wild Version

For a taste "on the wild side"— substitute the white rice with a package of wild rice cooked per package instructions. Add chopped water chestnuts to compliment the casserole's crunchiness.

Two bunches fresh broccoli, washed and
cut into small flowerets
6 cups salted, boiling water
½ cup chopped onion
½ cup butter, melted
1⅓ cups cooked white rice
One 8-ounce jar Cheddar processed cheese spread
One 10½-ounce can cream of mushroom soup

Cook broccoli in salted boiling water for 5 minutes. Drain thoroughly. Combine broccoli, onions, butter, rice, cheese, and soup in a large casserole lightly sprayed with cooking spray. Bake at 350 degrees for 30 minutes.

8 servings

One 10-ounce package frozen chopped broccoli can be substituted for fresh broccoli; thaw, no need to cook before adding to casserole.

Sunny Summer Squash Casserole

2 Tablespoons butter
¼ cup crumbled butter-flavored crackers
¼ cup chopped pecans
¼ cup water
½ teaspoon salt
1 pound yellow squash, sliced
¼ cup mayonnaise
1 egg, beaten
½ cup shredded Cheddar cheese
2 Tablespoons melted butter
1½ teaspoons sugar
¼ to ½ teaspoon minced onion

Microwave butter in a 1-quart casserole until melted. Add crumbs and pecans, and microwave for 1 minute. Stir mixture, and microwave for 1 minute. Pour crumb mixture onto wax paper and set aside. Place water, salt, and squash in same casserole. Cover and microwave for 4 minutes. Stir squash, and microwave for 4 to 6 minutes, until squash is tender. Drain juice from casserole. Combine mayonnaise, egg, cheese, melted butter, sugar, and minced onion in bowl. Pour mayonnaise mixture over squash and mix gently in casserole. Top with crumb mixture. Microwave at medium power 2 to 4 minutes more, until center is set. Let stand 5 minutes before serving.

Harvest Sweet Potato Casserole

Two 29-ounce cans sweet potatoes, drained and mashed
1 cup light brown sugar
2 eggs, beaten
½ stick margarine
¾ cup milk
½ teaspoon nutmeg
½ teaspoon cinnamon

Mix ingredients together in large mixing bowl until thoroughly blended. Place in 9 x 13-inch baking dish. Bake at 400 degrees for 25 minutes. Remove from oven. Sprinkle topping over baked potatoes evenly. Return to oven to crisp and brown topping, approximately 20 minutes.

Topping

½ cup light brown sugar
½ stick margarine
½ cup finely chopped pecans

Crumble ingredients together in a mixing bowl. Place over baked sweet potato casserole so that when melted topping will cover potatoes. Return casserole to oven for 20 minutes, until brown and bubbly.

12 servings

Traditional Cornbread Dressing

Two 14½-ounce cans chicken broth
One 8-inch round cornbread, cooked and crumbled
3-4 slices stale white bread, torn into pieces
1 medium onion, ends and outer skins removed,
chopped finely
2 celery stalks, chopped finely
2 eggs, beaten
1 teaspoon sage
½ teaspoon salt
1 teaspoon pepper

Preheat oven to 300 degrees. Coat 9 x 13-inch casserole with cooking spray, set aside. Heat chicken broth in saucepan on high heat to boiling point. Remove from heat. Combine crumbled cornbread, bread pieces, onion, and celery in mixing bowl. Add eggs, sage, salt, and pepper to cornbread mixture and mix well. Stir in hot chicken broth until mixed well. Put into casserole evenly. Bake in oven at 300 degrees for 35 minutes, or until golden light brown. Serve hot with turkey, chicken, or ham.

Berries & Nuts Dressing

A tasty dressing with bird or game meat dishes.

One 8-inch round day-old cornbread
6 cups bread crumbs
1 cup pecan pieces
1 teaspoon sage
One 16-ounce can whole cranberry sauce
½ cup melted margarine
1 egg, beaten

Crumble cornbread, and combine with bread crumbs, nuts, and sage. Stir in cranberry sauce, margarine, and egg; gently mix. Pour into 9 x 13-inch casserole. Bake at 350 degrees for 45 minutes.

10 servings

Grilling

Veggie Burgers

Delicious and very satisfying. Utilize the vegetable pulp leftover when juicing to create interesting combinations for patties like this.

2 eggs
⅓ cup plain yogurt
2 teaspoons Worcestershire sauce
2 teaspoons curry powder
½ teaspoon salt
¼ teaspoon ground red pepper
1⅓ cups cooked couscous
½ cup finely chopped walnuts
½ cup grated carrot
½ cup minced green onions
⅓ cup bread crumbs
4 sesame seed hamburger buns
Honey mustard
Hamburger pickles

Combine eggs, yogurt, Worcestershire sauce, curry powder, salt, and red pepper in bowl. Beat until well blended. Stir in couscous, walnuts, carrots, green onions, and bread crumbs. Mix well. Shape into 4 patties. Spray grill with cooking spray and place patties directly on rack. Grill over medium-high for 10 to 12 minutes, turning after 5 or 6 minutes. Serve on toasted buns with mustard and pickles.

Cooked rice may be substituted for couscous.

Crunchy Hash Browns

1 stick margarine
6 cups finely shredded, peeled white potatoes
1 teaspoon salt
½ teaspoon paprika
¼ teaspoon pepper

Melt margarine in nonstick skillet over medium heat. Form potatoes into patties and cook for 10 minutes, covered. Sprinkle with
salt, paprika, and pepper. Cook another 15 minutes, turning with
spatula occasionally until both sides are lightly browned. Remove
patties from heat and place on paper towels to drain.

When drained and cooled, place patties in layers of wax paper, and
put in airtight container for freezer. Freeze until ready to grill. To
prepare on grill, remove from wax paper wrappings and place on
top rack of grill over medium heat. Brown both sides, approximately 2 minutes each side. Serve hot.

Grilled Cabbage

1 large head cabbage
1 to 2 Tablespoons butter, optional
Salt, to taste
Pepper, to taste
5 or 6 small red potatoes

A dish that is so delicious, that boiled cabbage may be served only when weather is at its worst!

Spread out two layers of aluminum foil, approximately the size of a serving platter. Spray with a heavy coat of cooking spray. Cut washed cabbage head into one inch slices, removing core. Lay slices flat on one layer of aluminum foil. Spray lightly with cooking spray. Wash red potatoes and slice into thick rounds. Lay potatoes on top of cabbage layer. Spray with cooking spray, or dot with butter. Salt and pepper lightly. Cover with layer of aluminum foil, folding up edges to seal foil packet. Place packet on grill rack. Grill should be on high heat. Grill for 35 minutes. Reduce heat to low and grill packet for another 10 to 15 minutes. Keep warm on upper tier of grill rack, until other grilled items are ready to serve.

4 to 6 servings

Grilled Corn on the Cob

6 ears of fresh corn with husks
1 quart water
Butter

Trim outer, dry husks and excess corn silk from corn ears, leaving clean green husks intact on ears. Soak ears in water for 30 minutes, turning occasionally to make sure that all sides are equally soaked. Remove ears from water and allow to drain. Place directly on top grill rack over medium heat for 20 to 30 minutes, turning every 5 minutes. Time of cooking also depends upon other items in grill. Shuck husks and remove cornsilk before serving with butter or spray.

Don's Hot Sauce

1 quart red cider vinegar
1½ ounces salt
1½ ounces red cayenne pepper

Place all ingredients in covered container. Refrigerate overnight. Shake well before each use.

This sauce is great with barbecued meats—pork, beef, chicken, and mutton. My father prepared this sauce every summer when we were visited by out-of-state relatives, all of whom would request Kentucky barbecue for our family get-together meal.

Grilled Sweet Onion

One large Vidalia onion
½ teaspoon salt
1 teaspoon prepared horseradish
1 Tablespoon mayonnaise

This is a delicious side whenever serving grilled meat.

Clean onion, removing flaky outer skins. Cut onion in half through middle. Spray inner sides with cooking spray. Place directly on top grill rack and cook over medium heat for 15 minutes. Remove and cut each side into quarters, and sprinkle with salt while hot. Combine horseradish and mayonnaise in small serving bowl. Serve as dip with onion.

2 servings

Grilled Yellow Squash

4 large yellow squash
½ teaspoon lemon pepper
½ teaspoon salt

Wash yellow squash with cold water and drain. Cut in half lengthwise. Spray inner side with cooking spray. Sprinkle with lemon pepper and salt. Place face down on top grill rack over medium heat. Cook for 10 minutes. Serve hot.

8 servings

Terrific Chicken Kabobs

1 pound boneless and skinless chicken breasts
1 large red pepper
1 orange, thinly sliced in rounds with rinds
One 10-ounce carton mushrooms
One 14-ounce can pineapple chunks
2 Tablespoons teriyaki sauce
2 Tablespoons orange juice concentrate
1 teaspoon sesame seeds
½ teaspoon crushed red pepper
Orange slices with rinds, for garnish
½ teaspoon salt

Delicious served with rice and scallions.

Cut chicken and red pepper into 1½-inch pieces. Drain pineapple chunks; reserve juice. Alternately thread chicken, pepper, mushrooms, and pineapple chunks on skewers. Combine teriyaki sauce, orange juice concentrate, sesame seeds, crushed red pepper, and pineapple juice in long flat pan. Lay each skewer in pan with juices, and turn to coat each side with juice mixture. Twist a slice of orange and thread on end of each skewer. Place skewers on medium high grill for 10 to 12 minutes, turning each once during grilling. Remove from grill and season sparingly with salt. Serve on plates with or without skewers.

4 servings

Lucky Turkey

One 12-pound turkey
4 Tablespoons lemon pepper
2 Tablespoons chopped fresh parsley
1 Tablespoon celery salt
2 cloves garlic, minced
2 teaspoons coarsely ground black pepper
1 teaspoon sage
1 medium yellow onion, cut into 8 wedges
1 carrot, thinly sliced
1 apple, cored and cut into 8 wedges

The night before cooking, completely clean and dry outside and inside of turkey. Mix together lemon pepper, parsley, celery salt, garlic, black pepper, and sage. Rub seasonings over outer and inner surfaces of turkey. Cover and set in refrigerator overnight. The day of cooking remove turkey from refrigerator and stuff with onion wedges, carrot, and apple wedges. Tie wings and legs close to the body with cooking string. Secure turkey on rotisserie skewer. Place drip pan in grill with enough water to half fill pan. Cook turkey over medium heat for approximately 2 hours, or until internal temperature of turkey reaches 185 degrees.

Orange Ginger Ham

¼ cup frozen orange juice concentrate, thawed
¼ cup dry white wine
1 teaspoon dry mustard
¼ teaspoon ground ginger
One 2-pound cooked center cut ham slice,
1 to 1½-inch thick
6 pineapple slices, may be canned or fresh

Combine orange juice, wine, mustard, and ginger in small bowl. Cut slashes in ham slice and brush liberally with juice mixture. Grill directly on rack over medium for 10 minutes, brushing with juice mixture. Grill pineapple slices beside ham, also brushing with juice mixture. Flip ham slice, place pineapple slices on top, and brush with juice mixture. Grill 10 more minutes.

6 servings

Grilled Pineapple Rings

¼ cup pineapple juice
2 Tablespoons brown sugar
Fresh pineapple rings, each 1-inch thick

Serve with chicken, pork, or vegetarian meals.

Mix juice and sugar, stir until sugar dissolves. Brush pineapple rings with juice mixture, and place rings on grill. Cook on medium until light golden then flip and cook other side about 30 seconds.

111

Poolside Pizza

1½ teaspoons dry yeast
1 cup lukewarm water
½ teaspoon sugar
3 cups all-purpose flour
3 Tablespoons olive oil
¼ cup tomato paste
6 ounces sliced salami
1 red pepper, roasted, skinned and thinly sliced
¾ cup pitted black olives
8 ounces grated mozzarella cheese

My husband Bruce has been very helpful with the grilling recipes, and he must take credit for his expertise in working with bread and pizza dough. This pizza can easily become a veggie pizza by substituting the salami with sliced mushrooms, green peppers, and/or green olives.

Combine yeast, water, and sugar together in bowl. Let stand in a warm place until a foam appears. Combine yeast mixture with flour and oil in mixing bowl to form a dough. Knead on a lightly-floured surface; form a dough loaf. Cover and let stand in a warm place until doubled in size. Punch dough and roll out to the size of a barbecue pan. Lightly oil the pan and place dough in its base. Spread tomato paste over dough base and top with salami, red peppers, olives, and cheese. Place pan on grill over medium heat for approximately 30 minutes. Keep watch to prevent dough from burning. Setting the pan indirectly over heat prevents burning the dough base before the toppings are nicely done.

Honey Herbed Pork Roast

1 cup beer
½ cup honey
½ cup Dijon mustard
¼ cup olive oil
½ small onion, finely chopped
1 clove garlic, minced
2 teaspoons dried rosemary
½ teaspoon salt
¼ teaspoon ground black pepper
3 pounds pork loin roast
1 large yellow onion, thinly sliced

Combine beer, honey, mustard, oil, onion, garlic, rosemary, salt, and pepper in bowl and blend to make a marinade. Put pork into plastic bag with marinade and seal. Marinate at least 4 hours in refrigerator. Remove pork to grill and reserve marinade to use as baste. Wrap pork with foil and grill on medium heat for approximately 1½ hours. Baste frequently with marinade, opening foil and resealing each time you baste. Add onion to pork in foil packet during last 15 minutes of grilling.

Best BLT

One pound thick-sliced bacon
12 to 16 slices white bread, toasted
2 large red tomatoes, peeled and sliced
8 large lettuce leaves, cleaned and patted dry
¼ cup mayonnaise

E*njoy!*

For each sandwich, thread 2 or 3 slices of bacon per grilling skewers. Place on top rack of uncovered grill over medium heat and cook approximately 15 minutes, turning at least once. Cook to desired doneness. Remove from skewers and arrange bacon on one slice of sandwich toast. Over bacon slices place tomato slices, then lettuce. Spread mayonnaise thinly on remaining toast and place spread side down on top of bacon sandwich. Serve as whole sandwiches or slice in two.

Leg of Lamb

1½ cups red wine
1 onion, chopped
1 carrot, chopped
1 rib celery, chopped
2 Tablespoons chopped parsley
2 Tablespoons olive oil
3 cloves garlic, minced
1 Tablespoon dried thyme
1 teaspoon salt
1 teaspoon black pepper
1½ pounds boneless leg of lamb

As lovely as the month of May; delicious served with grilled pineapple.

Combine, wine, onion, carrot, celery, parsley, olive oil, garlic, thyme, salt, and pepper in bowl. Place leg of lamb in large resealable plastic bag. Add wine mixture to bag. Marinate in refrigerator overnight, or a minimum of 2 hours. Drain lamb; reserve marinade. Place lamb directly on grill over drip pan. Grill over medium heat for 45 minutes, turning occasionally to prevent burning. Brush liberally with marinade every 10 minutes. Discard unused marinade. Slice generously before serving.

4 servings

Steaks with Herb Mustard

Two 1-inch boneless ribeye steaks
2 large garlic cloves, crushed
2 teaspoons water
2 Tablespoons Dijon mustard
½ teaspoon black pepper
½ teaspoon dried thyme leaves
Salt to taste

Trim fat from steaks; set aside. Mix together garlic and water in microwave-able bowl. Microwave 30 seconds on high. Stir mustard, pepper, and thyme into garlic water, and blend. Spread mustard sauce on both sides of both steaks. Place steaks over medium heat on grill for approximately 12 minutes, turning about halfway through cooking time. Salt after removing from grill, if desired.

Riverboat Roast

4 pound beef pot roast
1 teaspoon grated lemon peel
½ cup lemon juice
⅓ cup cooking oil
2 Tablespoons sliced green onions
4 teaspoons sugar
1½ teaspoon salt
1 teaspoon Worcestershire sauce
1 teaspoon prepared mustard
⅛ teaspoon black pepper

Slice roast meat into 2-inch slices. Score edges with knife and place in shallow baking dish.

Combine lemon peel, lemon juice, oil, onions, sugar, and salt in bowl and mix. Pour lemon mixture over roast. Cover dish and refrigerate overnight. Turn meat over several times during the night. Remove roast from dish and reserve marinade. Grill roast slices over medium heat 12 to 15 minutes. Turn over and cook 12 to 15 minutes. Combine Worcestershire sauce, mustard and pepper with marinade and simmer in saucepan for 10 minutes. Place roast meat on serving platter and spoon marinade over top of meat.

6 to 8 servings

Hickory Smoked Catfish Filets

The catfish is a great sporting fish that populates the state's lakes. Kentucky lake catfish is widely known as a popular fried fish. This version offers an alternative, delicious preparation. Filets are commonly available in the fish and seafood sections of most supermarkets.

Hickory chips
2 Tablespoons olive oil
1 clove garlic, minced
2 Tablespoons lemon juice
1 teaspoon grated lemon peel
½ teaspoon dried dill weed
½ teaspoon dried thyme
¼ teaspoon salt
¼ teaspoon black pepper
Four 5-ounce catfish filets

Soak hickory chips in water for 1 hour. Combine olive oil, garlic, lemon juice, lemon peel, and seasonings together in bowl. Marinate filets in mixture for 15 minutes Drain water from hickory chips and put chips in grill per manufacturer's instructions. Place filets on grill or fish tray for grill. Grill fish for 3 minutes over medium high heat on each side. Brush marinade over filets while cooking.

Desserts

Apple Dumplings

A lways a
   delectable
dessert.

8 large apples, peeled and sliced
1 teaspoon nutmeg
1 teaspoon cinnamon
1 stick and 1 Tablespoon margarine, divided
1 cup plus 3 Tablespoons sugar, divided
¼ cup water
1 cup all-purpose flour
1 teaspoon baking powder
½ teaspoon salt
2 to 3 Tablespoons milk

Place apples in a saucepan with nutmeg, cinnamon, 1 stick margarine, and 1 cup sugar. Add water, cover and cook over medium heat until apples are tender. Stir occasionally while cooking to prevent sticking. While apples cook put 1 cup flour, baking powder, salt, 3 tablespoons sugar, and 1 tablespoon margarine in a large mixing bowl. Cut margarine into dry ingredients until the consistency of cornmeal. Add milk by spoonful as necessary to make a stiff dough. Lightly coat baking casserole with cooking spray. Pour cooked apple mixture into baking dish, spreading to cover dish bottom. Drop dough by teaspoonfuls on top of hot apples. Bake uncovered at 425 degrees for 15 to 20 minutes, or until dumplings are brown. Allow to cool slightly before serving, as hot apple syrup can burn the tongue and lips.

8 servings

Peaches 'n Cream Pie

1 cup sugar
One 8-ounce package cream cheese, room temperature
One 8-ounce container whipped topping,
room temperature
3 to 4 large fresh peaches, peeled and pitted
1 graham cracker pie shell

Combine sugar and cream cheese in bowl. Cream with hand mixer on high speed. Stir in whipped topping; mix on low speed until blended. Cut peaches into bite-size pieces. Layer peaches in bottom of crust. Pour cream mixture on top of peaches. Spread evenly to cover. Cover pie with lid. Refrigerate overnight. The pie may also be frozen; thaw before serving.

This is a light, refreshing summer dessert, which can be made with reduced fat crust, cream cheese, and whipped topping. Caution: do not use fat free cream cheese because it will not blend well with sugar.

Summer Strawberry Pie

1 quart fresh strawberries
1 cup sugar
3 Tablespoons cornstarch
1 cup hot water
1 Tablespoon butter
½ teaspoon lemon juice
Red food coloring
One baked 9-inch pie shell
Whipped topping

Wash strawberries in cold running water; remove stems and caps. Allow to drain. Slice some berries if desired, but leave most whole for pie; set aside. Cook sugar, and cornstarch in hot water in a small saucepan until thick. Add butter, lemon juice, and red food coloring to hot mixture. Place berries in pie shell. Pour hot sugar mixture over berries; cover loosely and set aside to cool. When cooled keep in refrigerator until ready to serve. Beautifully served with whipped topping.

8 servings

Cousin's Coconut Pie

2 eggs, beaten
1 cup sugar
½ cup melted margarine
1 teaspoon vanilla
1 cup flaked coconut
½ cup chopped pecans
Unbaked 9-inch pie shell

This quickly pre-
pared dessert is a
nice welcome for visi-
tors, or a
neighborly chat.

Combine eggs, sugar, margarine, vanilla, coconut, and pecans in bowl and mix well. Pour into pie shell. Bake at 350 degrees for 45 minutes.

Holiday Lemon Pie

A delectable dessert for holidays and special occasions.

3 Tablespoons margarine, divided
¼ cup firmly-packed brown sugar
One 8½-ounce can crushed pineapple, well drained
¼ cup flaked coconut
One unbaked 9-inch pie crust
1 can prepared lemon pie filling
Whipped topping
2 Tablespoons toasted coconut

Melt 2 Tablespoons margarine, and mix with sugar, pineapple, and flaked coconut. Spread over bottom of crust. Bake at 425 degrees for 15 minutes, until pastry is golden and pineapple layer is bubbly. Remove from oven and cool on rack. Melt 1 Tablespoon margarine. Blend with pie filling. Pour filling over pineapple layer in crust. Swirl spoonfuls of whipped topping around edges of pie. Sprinkle whipped swirls with toasted coconut.

Commonwealth Chess Pie

3 egg yolks
1 cup milk
¾ cup sugar
½ cup margarine, melted
2 Tablespoons all-purpose flour
1 teaspoon vanilla
One 9-inch baked pie shell

This classic may be served while warm or if refrigerated, served chilled with a dollop of whipped topping and a sprinkle of nutmeg.

Combine egg yolks, milk, sugar, margarine, flour, and vanilla in top of double boiler. Bring water in boiler to a boil, while stirring top pan constantly. When mixture begins to thicken to a custard consistency, turn burner off. Continue to stir for 2 minutes, then allow to set for 5 minutes. Pour the custard into a baked pie shell.

Kentucky Pie

1 cup sugar
½ cup all-purpose flour
2 eggs, beaten
1 stick margarine, melted
1 teaspoon vanilla
1 cup semi-sweet chocolate chips
¾ cup finely-chopped pecans
½ cup shredded coconut
One unbaked 9-inch pie shell

A famous pie that has become a tradition for Derby parties. The Kentucky Derby horse race is dubbed "the greatest two minutes in sports."

Blend sugar, flour, eggs, margarine, and vanilla in large mixing bowl. Stir in chocolate chips, pecans, and coconut. Pour into pie shell evenly. Bake at 350 degrees for 30 to 35 minutes until firm.

Coffee Custard

1 teaspoon instant coffee
1½ cups sugar, divided
6 eggs
2¼ cups milk
½ cup coffee-flavored liqueur
¼ teaspoon salt
Dark chocolate shavings

Grease 8 custard cups. Stir together coffee granules and ¾ cup sugar in small saucepan over medium heat until smooth. Pour into custard cups. Beat eggs and ¾ cup sugar in mixing bowl until blended. Add milk, liqueur, and salt and beat well. Pour mixture into custard cups. Place custard cups in roasting pan with water to reach halfway up outer sides of cups. Bake at 350 degrees for 1 hour. A knife inserted in center of custard should come out clean. Carefully remove custard cups from pan. Cover and chill 3 hours. Before serving, invert onto dessert plates and garnish with chocolate shavings if desired.

8 servings

Bourbon Chocolate Cheesecake

V ery rich and distinctive.

6 chocolate wafers, finely crushed
1½ cups cream cheese
1 cup sugar
1 cup 1% low fat cottage cheese
¼ cup plus 2 Tablespoons cocoa
¼ cup all-purpose flour
¼ cup bourbon
1 teaspoon vanilla extract
¼ teaspoon salt
1 egg
2 Tablespoons semisweet chocolate mini-morsels
Fresh mint sprigs, for garnish

Preheat oven to 300 degrees. Sprinkle chocolate wafer crumbs into bottom of springform pan. Blend cream cheese, sugar, cottage cheese, cocoa, flour, bourbon, vanilla extract, and salt until smooth. Mix in egg until just blended. Fold in chocolate morsels. Pour mixture into pan.   Gently place in oven. Bake at 300 degrees 45 to 50 minutes, until set. Allow cake to cool in pan on wire rack. Cover and chill in refrigerator 8 to 10 hours. Remove sides of pan and transfer to serving plate. Garnish with mint sprigs.

16 servings

Kentucky Butter Cake

2 sticks butter
2 cups granulated sugar
4 eggs
1 cup buttermilk
2 teaspoons vanilla
3 cups all-purpose flour, sifted

Cream butter and sugar in large mixing bowl. Blend in eggs, one at a time, beating well with each one. Add buttermilk and vanilla to butter mixture, stir well. Add flour gradually, stirring well. Turn into 10-inch tube pan which has been greased on the bottom. Bake at 350 degrees for 1 hour. Remove from oven, place on rack to cool. Run spatula edge along sides and ends, and prick cake with a fork. Pour Kentucky Butter Cake Sauce over cake. Allow to set 2 hours before serving.

8 servings

Kentucky Butter Cake Butter Sauce

1 cup granulated sugar
¼ cup water
½ cup butter
1 teaspoon rum extract

Combine sugar, water, and butter in saucepan. Heat until melted, but not boiling. Add rum extract, remove from heat. Pour over warm cake while sauce is hot.

Family Reunion Carrot Cake

This wonderful cake is great for the family or taken to gatherings. The cake may also be prepared in three 9–inch round layer cake pans if a layer cake is desired. Use frosting between layers, as well as on sides and top of cake.

2 cups all-purpose flour, sifted
2 teaspoons baking powder
1½ teaspoons baking soda
2 teaspoons cinnamon
1½ teaspoons salt
2 cups sugar
1½ cups salad oil
4 eggs
2 cups finely grated carrots
One 8½-ounce can crushed pineapple
½ cup chopped walnuts
One 3½-ounce can flaked coconut

Sift together flour, baking powder, baking soda, cinnamon, and salt in large mixing bowl. Add sugar, oil, and eggs and beat well. Blend in carrots, pineapple, walnuts, and coconut. Pour into 9 x 13-inch baking pan which has been lightly greased and floured. Bake at 325 degrees for 35 minutes. Remove from oven to cool. Frost with Cream Cheese Frosting.

12 servings

Cream Cheese Frosting

½ cup butter, softened
One 8-ounce package cream cheese, softened
1 teaspoon vanilla extract
1 pound confectioner's sugar

Cream together butter, cream cheese, and vanilla in mixing bowl.
Add sugar gradually, beating well. If too thick to spread smoothly,
thin with a teaspoon or two of milk.

Picnic Chocolate Cake

2 cups sugar
2 cups all-purpose flour
⅓ cup cocoa
1 teaspoon baking soda
½ teaspoon salt
2 sticks margarine
1 cup water
½ cup buttermilk
2 eggs
1 teaspoon pure vanilla

Mix dry ingredients. Heat margarine and water until boiling; pour over dry ingredients. Beat in buttermilk, eggs, and vanilla. Pour batter into greased and floured 15 x 10-inch pan. Bake at 400 degrees for 20 minutes. Top with icing while hot.

Icing

1 stick margarine
¼ cup cocoa
6 Tablespoons milk
4 cups powdered sugar
1 cup chopped walnuts

Combine margarine, cocoa, and milk in saucepan. Heat to boiling. Combine sugar and nuts in mixing bowl. Pour hot margarine mixture over sugar and nuts; mix well. Spread on hot cake.

German Chocolate Upside Down Cake

1 cup chopped walnuts
1 cup shredded coconut
1 box German chocolate cake mix
1 stick margarine, melted and cooled
1 box powdered sugar
8 ounces cream cheese

A fine contemporary version of a traditional dessert.

Grease and flour 9 x 13-inch baking pan. Sprinkle chopped nuts evenly over bottom. Sprinkle coconut evenly over chopped nuts. Mix cake mix as directed on box. Spoon over nuts and coconut. Beat margarine, sugar, and cream cheese together until smooth. Spoon over cake mix layer. Bake at 350 degrees for 45 minutes. Do not overcook.

Glorious Orange Cake

1 cup shortening
2 cups sugar
4 eggs, separated
½ teaspoon salt
1 teaspoon baking soda
3½ cups all-purpose flour
1⅓ cups buttermilk
Two 8-ounce packages chopped dates
1 cup pecan pieces
2 Tablespoons grated orange peel

Cream shortening and sugar in mixing bowl. Add egg yolks and beat well. Add salt, baking soda, flour, and buttermilk. Mix well. Fold in dates, pecans, and orange peel. Mix well. Fold in stiffly beaten egg whites. Pour into a bundt or angel food pan. Bake at 350 degrees for 30 minutes. Do not remove cake from pan. While cake is hot, puncture liberally and drizzle with topping. Turn out onto a large sheet of foil. Cool cake completely. Bring foil sides up and over top of cake to make airtight. Store for 3 or 4 days before serving.

Topping

2 cups sugar
¾ cup orange juice
¼ cup rum

Mix together in bowl and set aside 30 minutes.

Walnut Bourbon Balls

2½ cups finely ground vanilla wafers
1 cup confectioner's sugar
1 cup finely-chopped walnuts
2 Tablespoons cocoa
¼ cup bourbon
3 Tablespoons corn syrup
1 cup granulated sugar

An easy, no–bake treat with a very sweet, distinctive flavor, very Kentuckian.

Mix vanilla wafers, confectioner's sugar, walnuts, and cocoa. Add bourbon and corn syrup, mixing well. Roll into 1-inch balls, and roll each ball in granulated sugar. Store in air tight container. Refrigerate several days before serving.

Approximately 3 dozen candies

Buttermilk Sherbet

1 quart buttermilk
½ cup sugar
1½ cups light corn syrup
½ cup lemon or lime juice
2 Tablespoons grated lemon rind
½ teaspoon vanilla

Placing a miniature marshmallow in the bottom of a sugar ice cream cone helps prevent unwanted drips, and offers a sweet finale.

Mix all the ingredients together in a large bowl. Beat with mixer on medium speed about 2 minutes. Pour mixture into ice cube trays. Freeze until edges are firm. Turn cubes out into a cooled mixing bowl. Beat with mixer on low speed until smooth. Cover tightly and return to freezer for 1 hour. Remove from freezer and beat with mixer on low speed for 2 minutes. Cover and return to freezer for 1 hour. Remove from freezer and beat with mixer on low speed for 1 minute. Cover and return to freezer until frozen to desired hardness.

Makes 1½ quarts.

Winter Strawberries

Two 3-ounce packages strawberry gelatin
1 cup ground pecans
1 cup flaked coconut
¾ cup sweetened condensed milk
½ teaspoon vanilla extract
Pink decorative sugar
green food coloring
½ cup water
½ cup sliced almonds

A delightful candy to surprise family and guests during winter festivities.
Very elegant when served on a silver tray with a white paper doily.

Mix gelatin, pecans, coconut, condensed milk, and vanilla extract in bowl. Refrigerate 1 hour. Form strawberries by pinching a small amount about the size of a strawberry from the chilled gelatin dough. Shape into the form of a strawberry with a small indentation at the top for the stem. Roll each in pink decorative sugar; refrigerate aside. Add green food coloring to water to make desired shade of green for stems. Soak almond slices in green water for 10 minutes, then remove from water and place on paper towels to absorb excess water. Place one almond slice in top indentation of each strawberry.

20-25 pieces

Wedding Mints

These can be kept a couple of weeks or frozen in an air–tight container. Refreshing and good for mixers, weddings, and receptions.

3 Tablespoons butter, softened
¼ cup cream
¼ cup salt
1 teaspoon vanilla
2 teaspoons peppermint extract
1 pound confectioner's sugar
Food coloring

Mix all ingredients except food coloring in mixing bowl. Knead until smooth. Add food coloring if desired, mix evenly. Roll mixture into small balls. Place on waxed paper. Dip fork in confectioner's sugar and press each ball. Allow to set overnight. Store in air tight container.

50 mints

Kentucky
Kids
Cook

Splitter Splatters (Hipp Cakes)

A family tradition—"Splitter Splatters" were a Saturday morning treat for my cousins and me while visiting my grandmother, "Mama Juel" Winstead Hipp. We would help cook, and they always tasted better than anything in the world!!

1 to 2 Tablespoons butter
2 large eggs
2 Tablespoon sugar
1 Tablespoon baking powder
¼ teaspoon salt
One 3½-ounce can evaporated milk
1 cup sifted all-purpose flour
3 Tablespoons water
Maple syrup, warmed

Melt butter in large flat skillet on medium heat. Break eggs into large mixing bowl. Pour sugar on eggs, and beat with fork. Add baking powder and salt, and beat again. Pour in whole can of evaporated milk, and beat. Gradually add flour while beating with fork until thick, smooth consistency. Thin with 1 to 3 tablespoons water. Spoon onto skillet, making "splitter splatter" designs. Flip with spatula when bubbles appear on surface of pancake. Cook side for a minute, or until lightly browned. Serve immediately, with syrup.

These may also be cooked as pancakes.

This recipe makes 4 to 6 large pancakes.

Milk Toast

1 piece white bread, toasted,
buttered, torn into bite-size pieces
1 cup milk
1 Tablespoon sugar
¼ teaspoon cinnamon

A kid's favorite, especially soothing during sore throat season.

Put buttered toast pieces into a flat bowl or cereal dish. Heat milk, sugar, and cinnamon in small saucepan until very warm. Careful not to burn or boil! Pour milk mixture over toast. Serve immediately.

1 serving

Trail Mix

A convenient treat for rest stops when on the "trail."

1 cup toasted oatmeal cereal
1 cup sun-dried raisins
1 cup candy coated chocolate candies
1 cup miniature marshmallows
1 cup shelled peanuts, almonds, or sunflower seeds

Combine all ingredients. Store in airtight plastic container or plastic bags.

8 to 10 servings

Carrot Raisin Salad

¼ cup raisins
1 cup grated carrots
3 Tablespoons nonfat yogurt
1 Tablespoon mayonnaise
¼ teaspoon cinnamon
¼ teaspoon pepper
1 teaspoon orange juice concentrate

A healthy and easy salad for everyone.

Toss raisins and carrots into bowl. In another bowl combine yogurt, mayonnaise, cinnamon, pepper, and orange juice. Stir yogurt mixture into carrots and raisins; mix well. Cover and refrigerate to chill.

Firecracker Candy Apples

8 small red delicious apples
8 wooden ice cream sticks
3 cups sugar
½ cup corn syrup
¼ cup red-hot candies
½ teaspoon red food coloring
1 cup water

Hard ball stage is reached when a small amount of mixture dropped into very cold water becomes a hard ball or string.

Wash and dry apples. Insert wooden sticks into each through the stem end. Heat sugar, corn syrup, red-hot candies, food coloring, and water in a saucepan over medium heat. Stir frequently until sugar and candies are dissolved. Boil until mixture reaches hard ball stage. Remove from heat and dip apples on sticks into hot candy mixture. Swirl to coat evenly. Place apples on greased baking sheet to cool at least an hour before eating.

Red, White, and Blue Salute

One 8-ounce carton nonfat whipped topping
1 cup strawberries, thickly sliced
1 cup blueberries

Cover bottom of 4 clear sundae cups with ½ inch of whipped topping. Spoon a layer of strawberries onto whipped topping. Spread a thin layer of whipped topping on top of strawberry layer. Spoon a layer of blueberries onto whipped topping layer. Place a dollop of whipped topping on top of each cup.

Adorn with small American flags on long toothpicks for a patriotic flair.

Bacon Peanut Butter Rollups

Thin sliced bacon
Whole wheat bread, , crust trimmed off
Creamy peanut butter

Cut slices of bacon in half, place on broiling rack or microwave plate. Broil or microwave until half done. Drain bacon on a paper towel. Spread bread with thin coat of peanut butter. Cut bread into slices the width of bacon. Roll up bread slices, then wrap each roll with a bacon slice. Secure bacon wrap with a toothpick. Place rolls on broiler rack. Broil on medium heat, turning roll-ups to brown each on all sides.

Approximately 3 to 4 roll-ups per slice of bread

Brown Sugar Bumps

¼ cup butter
½ cup brown sugar
¼ cup peanut butter
1 cup regular oatmeal

Simple, sweet, and old fashioned.

Melt butter gently by putting in a cup, then placing in a pan of hot water. Do not let any water drip into the butter! Let the hot water slowly melt the butter in the cup, stir to aid the process. Pour melted butter into a large bowl. Add brown sugar to bowl; mix. Add peanut butter to bowl; mix. Add oatmeal to bowl; mix. Drop by spoonfuls onto waxed paper. Form with fingers into balls. Allow to set for 20 minutes.

Miss Ruth's Peanut Butter Cookies

A classic recipe, and an opportunity to let a child help with each step of preparation.

½ cup butter
½ cup peanut butter
½ cup sugar
½ cup packed brown sugar
1 egg
1¼ cups all-purpose flour

Cream together butter and peanut butter in large mixing bowl. Add sugar and brown sugar gradually. Add egg and flour. Mix ingredients thoroughly. Form dough into small balls. Place on ungreased cookie sheet. Press each ball with back of fork which has been dipped in flour. Bake at 375 degrees for 10-12 minutes.

Snicker Doodles

1 cup shortening
1½ cups sugar
2 eggs
2⅔ cups sifted all-purpose flour
3 teaspoons cream of tartar
1 teaspoon baking soda
¼ teaspoon salt
3 Tablespoons sugar
3 teaspoons cinnamon

These are cookie jar treats that stay crisp and tasty for days.

Preheat oven to 400 degrees. Combine shortening, sugar, eggs, flour, cream of tartar, baking soda, and salt. Roll into balls the size of a walnut and coat with mixture of sugar and cinnamon. Bake on an ungreased cookie sheet in 400 degree oven for 8 to 10 minutes.

Can't Eat Just One
Potato Chip Cookies

Even big kids love these!

1 cup margarine
½ cup sugar
1 teaspoon vanilla
½ cup crushed potato chips
½ cup chopped pecans
2 cups all-purpose flour, sifted

Cream margarine, sugar, and vanilla. Add potato chips and pecans. Stir in flour, mix thoroughly. Roll into ½-inch balls. Place on ungreased cookie sheet. Press each ball with bottom of glass that has been dipped in granulated sugar. Bake a t 350 degrees for 16 to 18 minutes, until lightly browned on bottom.

3 dozen cookies

Ranger Cookies

½ cup butter
½ cup granulated sugar
½ cup brown sugar
1 egg, beaten
1 cup all-purpose flour, sifted
½ teaspoon baking soda
½ teaspoon baking powder
½ teaspoon vanilla
Pinch salt
¼ cup coconut
1 cup oatmeal
½ cup Rice Krispies
½ cup pecans
½ cup raisins

These cookies are great fun for kids to make. Everyone may take a turn adding an ingredient, and mixing it into the cookie dough. Great to pack up as a snack for outdoor excursions.

Cream butter, white sugar, and brown sugar in large mixing bowl. Add egg, and mix well. Add flour, baking soda, baking powder, and vanilla. Mix well. Add salt, coconut, oatmeal, Rice Krispies, pecans, and raisins. Mix well. Drop by spoonfuls onto greased cookie sheet. Bake at 350 degrees for 12 to 15 minutes.

Nutty Fingers

6 Tablespoons plus half cup powdered sugar, divided
¾ cup melted butter, cooled
2 cups all-purpose flour
1 cup chopped pecans
1 teaspoon vanilla
Dash salt
1 teaspoon cold water

Combine sugar, butter, flour, pecans, vanilla, and salt in bowl. Add water if needed. Mix well and shape dough into fingers. Bake at 300 degrees for 45 minutes. Roll in powdered sugar when cooled.

Friday Fudge

One 11½ -ounce bag semi-sweet chocolate chips
One 16-ounce can chocolate cake frosting
½ cup chopped nuts

A super easy, smooth fudge, without the stirring!

Place chocolate chips in microwave-safe bowl and melt in microwave. Stir together melted chocolate and frosting in bowl. Add nuts, if desired. Pour into glass dish. Allow to set before cutting into squares.

Many thanks to those who provided photographs

Mrs. Julian Beatty

From the family photo album of Earl & Mildred McMurtrie Floyd

From the family photo album of Paul & Juel Winstead Hipp

Mr. Louis F. Kirchoff, Jr. of Kirchoff's Bakery

Lyon County Herald Ledger

Mrs. Joyce Mattingly

McCracken County Library

Mrs. Denee Sullivan

Mr. and Mrs. Barron White

Index

Grilling

Kentucky Kids Cook

Salads & Soups

Sides